CATCHING
THE
LIGHT

•

For Art:
Form is emptiness
+ emptiness is form.
Best,
Susan

July 1 1990

Catching the

THE

Light

SUSAN L. POPE

Susan L. Pope

VIKING

VIKING
Published by the Penguin Group
Viking Penguin, a division of Penguin Books USA Inc.,
375 Hudson Street, New York, New York 10014, U.S.A.
Penguin Books Ltd, 27 Wrights Lane, London W8 5TZ, England
Penguin Books Australia Ltd, Ringwood, Victoria, Australia
Penguin Books Canada Ltd, 2801 John Street,
Markham, Ontario, Canada L3R 1B4
Penguin Books (N.Z.) Ltd, 182–190 Wairau Road,
Auckland 10, New Zealand

Penguin Books Ltd, Registered Offices:
Harmondsworth, Middlesex, England

First published in 1990 by Viking Penguin,
a division of Penguin Books USA Inc.

1 3 5 7 9 10 8 6 4 2

Grateful acknowledgment is made for permission to
reprint an excerpt from "Stopping by Woods on a
Snowy Evening" from *The Poetry of Robert Frost* by
Edward Connery Lathem. Copyright 1923, 1969 by Holt,
Rinehart and Winston. Copyright 1951 by
Robert Frost. Reprinted by arrangement
with Henry Holt and Company, Inc.

LIBRARY OF CONGRESS CATALOGING IN PUBLICATION DATA
Pope, Susan L.
Catching the light / by Susan L. Pope.
p.   cm.
ISBN 0-670-83328-2
I. Title.
PS3566.O6263C38   1990
813'.54—dc20   89–40673

Printed in the United States of America
Set in Sabon

For my son, Aaron

ACKNOWLEDGMENTS

◆

The author wishes to thank her parents
for their support, Susan Dodd for believing
through the fallow years, The Millay Colony for
the Arts and Dorland Mountain Colony for time,
and Bonnie Maresh of the Waquoit Glass Works
for insights into the art of stained glass.

PART · I

Damaris—1959

When she was a child, folks in North Osprey who didn't know better called Damaris Bishop albino. True, she was light, her hair the bright gold sheen of the full moon, her skin all over as pale and translucent as the inside of your thigh. Then, too, she had the habit of wearing clothes lacking color: whites, creams, and soft yellows, in spite of her grandmother's efforts to get her into greens and pinks. She was indeed fair, but, as her eyes revealed, by no means albino. They were blue, blue as the marsh river seen against the marsh grass.

If folks were wrong about that, they were closer to the truth when they declared the girl a handful. "It's not right," they said, often enough behind Grand-pere Bishop's back, and they'd say it to his face, asked or not. Why, the Bishops were already old-timers when they took over the youngster's upbringing.

When, at the age of ten, Damaris skipped out on the Benovuccis's Fourth of July picnic without telling a soul where she was off to, it was no surprise to anyone. Although some feared she might have drowned in Osprey Harbor, to most

her behavior simply confirmed what Grand-pere often sput-
tered—she was an exasperating child.

That day she'd hitched to her favorite marsh off Route 6,
fifteen miles or so from North Osprey. She returned home
late and hungry. Faced with her grandparents' wrath and
punishment—grounded for two weeks—the child proclaimed
unfairness. They insisted. She swore and was sent to bed
without her supper.

An hour later her intent to run away for real had taken
her as far as the hollow between the scrub pine and the tulip
tree in the backyard. The broad, squat farmhouse before her
had once been a good distance from the village, but through
the years the village had spread up to the farm's front lawn.
Shingled in natural pine, weathered to a silvery-gray, the
house rested low and solid on its stone foundation. From
windows trimmed with deep red paint, light shone out into
the darkness and formed a tic-tac-toe pattern on the grass.

Pretty soon the old folks would begin their slow journey
down the hall across the wide floorboards that creaked like
old bones. Pretty soon Grandmother would lift the latch on
Damaris's door and peer in to see if she worked crossword
puzzles with the aid of the flashlight or ate cheese in the dark.
"Are you asleep?" the old woman whispered each night
through clacking false teeth, as if Damaris would answer
either way.

What's a nine-letter word for "Grandfather" in French?
———. Crossword puzzles. That's how Grandfather got his
nickname. They'd worked puzzles together since Damaris had
been a small child. At first she called him Grand-pere as a
joke, but then she grew to love the soft sound of the word.
For a time, he corrected her "*père*" with "father," but she
persisted. Eventually he relented and she thought he, too, had
secretly come to love the name, though she knew he'd never
admit it.

The evening dampness soaked through last year's thin summer pajamas. This year the pajama legs reached only to mid-calf and the buttons popped open across her chest. Under her bare feet the pine needles were as sharp and uncomfortable as her hunger. She closed her eyes and envisioned the green box of cocoa on the pantry shelf. The bitter chocolate in milk with a touch of sugar would soothe her. Maybe she should sneak back inside and fix a cup—tell them she couldn't sleep.

Never, no, never would she give in to them. She hated them—hated them. So slow and funny-looking in their old-fashioned clothes. Grand-pere wore his shoulder-length hair in a single braid down his back, and when he forgot to shave he resembled a scoundrel; Gabby Hayes or, worse, Long John Silver.

She crouched for what seemed like hours beneath the tree with the broad, six-pointed leaves. Suddenly the porch light went on and the back door opened with a *thwack*. Two flashlights beamed into the dark.

"Grandma can't take much more of this," the old woman hollered, clutching a sweater around her shoulders with one hand. Grand-pere repeated her name as he moved through the yard. His light flashed over the roses and tomatoes, skimmed the rope swing and a dilapidated shed. Damaris giggled and pressed her lips against her knee. Now it was fun—a party—a search party. Once more she had tricked them into concern, lured them into worry. Grandmother's light surprised her from behind.

"Over here, Franklin," the old woman called.

"Hey, now," Grand-pere said, and Damaris felt his rough, dry fingers against her arm as he tried to pull her out. She grasped a low pine branch; the hard, spiny bark twisted into her skin. With his free hand, Père touched her feet lightly. She squealed and wriggled and shouted *no!*, but the tickling continued. Her grip loosened and the old man dragged her out and jerked her to her feet. Before she could catch her breath he lifted her with arms strong and muscular from years of gardening and chopping wood. He flung her over his bony shoulder and strode across the grass to the house. Grandmother tripped behind, the spot from her flashlight zooming up and down like an electrified bat.

"What have you got to say for yourself?" Père asked with a tired voice, as he set her down in the tiny kitchen. Behind them the teakettle steamed and bubbled on the wood-fired cookstove. Silently Damaris removed a wad of sticky pine needles from the bottom of her foot.

"Impossible," Grandmother said, and with a swish of her polka-dotted skirt she left the girl and grandfather alone.

The room around them reflected the elder's diligent thrift. Years ago Grand-pere had handcrafted the beechwood drop-leaf table in his basement workshop. Painted gray with a border of white and pink rosa rugosa, it stood beneath the kitchen windows. Handmade knotty-pine cabinets held stacks of dishes on glass-fronted shelves. Grandmother's aprons hung on the pantry door. Inside, jars of rose-hip and beach-plum jam, canned tomatoes, green beans, and carrots from the summer garden lined the open shelves.

From beneath a scrim of hair Damaris peered at Père's black, high-lacing boots, at his cuffed pants, dark and patterned with gray stripes. "I'm waiting," he said every now and then, and she gazed a little higher along his form until at last she stared into his sharp, black, pinpointy eyes. The old eyes blinked.

"Exasperating child."

"Crusty old man."

Hands clasped her shoulders and shook her roughly a time or two. Tears came, but she would not cry, would not reveal any weakness, display any emotion in his presence. He turned her about and pushed her down the hall into her room. In her desire for his affection and concern she had managed only to antagonize him.

When the door closed between them she tiptoed to the mahogany highboy and felt along the corners of the bottom drawer. Beneath a stack of crossword-puzzle magazines she found a small wooden box. She turned the key on the bottom and when she lifted the lid "Frère Jacques" played. Singing along softly, she ran her fingers over the pattern of poppies burned into the wood long ago with a hot, metal rod. The box had belonged to Mitchell, her father.

Mitchell—1943

Mitchell Bishop bequeathed his parents, his home, and a sense of curiosity to his daughter. But what in Damaris was a vague, diffused interest in any number of things had been in Mitchell an obsession with sand; hot sand. An obsession that brought him rapping, at the age of fifteen, on the door of the glassblower, Italo Benovucci.

When no one answered that day, he entered uninvited. The old brick building had once been a station for the Cape Cod branch of the Old Colony Railroad. Mrs. Benovucci sat behind a wooden desk in a makeshift office just inside the door. With one hand she lifted a long braid of hair; with the other she wiped the moisture off her neck and face.

"I'm here to be apprenticed!" Mitchell shouted, over the roar of the furnace in the blowing room as sweat began to course down his back.

Mrs. Benovucci laughed. "You're too young. This work requires stamina, speed."

"I'm one of the fastest swimmers around," he admitted.

"This work requires strength," she said, as she forced open a recalcitrant desk drawer.

"I split an entire cord of wood single-handed." He failed to add that it had taken him several months.

"A miniature Paul Bunyan we have here." She set a black,

metal lunch box on the desktop with a clank. "We ask for teamwork."

"Two weeks on a fishing vessel. Cleaned everything from fish to scullery. Whatever the captain ordered," he said, with a salute. Well, he had gone deep-sea fishing once with his father.

"And now they call you Ishmael?" Mrs. Benovucci removed waxed paper from a *chouriço* sandwich. Red juice dripped down her fingers as she bit into the spicy sausage.

"And the hands," she said, "the hands and the eyes must be steady as . . . as . . ."

"A yogi's?"

"Yogi I don't know. Just steady is all."

Mitchell aligned his slim body and focused his eyes on the lunchbox. Then, with knees bent and arms extended firm and straight before him, he balanced on his toes.

Mrs. Benovucci put down her sandwich and stared.

"Youngsters today. Always something new."

Mitchell released the position and explained to Mrs. Benovucci, as she finished her lunch, that yoga was nothing new and in fact had been around for thousands of years. Had her lunch been larger, the brief history of yogic philosophy might have been longer, but midway through Mitchell's discourse she finished her sandwich, snapped the lunchbox shut, and motioned for the boy to follow her into the blowing room where Italo worked.

They descended several steps to the concrete floor of the studio. Wall fans energetically churned the heat-laden air. Shelves of wooden and metal tools lined the walls. Two small furnaces constructed of firebrick rested on metal tables.

"One furnace melts the glass," Mrs. Benovucci explained. "The second, the glory hole, is for reheating."

It took Mitchell's eyes a few seconds to adjust to the red-hot glow emitting from the glory hole, as if a sunbeam were trapped inside.

Italo, unlike his wife, had no questions for the boy. At fifteen, Benovucci himself had apprenticed in glassmaking at the famous Pairpoint Glass Company in New Bedford. After some years he opened his own shop on the west end of Cape Cod, far enough from New Bedford to avoid threat of competition.

Mitchell began work the next day; took his place at his makeshift workbench, a roughly hewn but tidy wooden stall. Forming tools rested on the seat beside him and on the shelf at his back. To his right was a low, metal-capped wood panel against which to rest the blowpipe as he shaped the glass. Buckets of water filled with forming tools and tins of crushed glass stood at his feet.

The boy became Italo's star pupil. For years afterward, Mrs. Benovucci claimed she knew instantly he was a prodigy, the very moment he came through the door.

Mitchell's early passion for glass evoked surprise from Osprey folks; his passion for Miss Stevenson evoked gossip. Twyla Stevenson, hired in 1944 as the new junior-high music teacher, had missed teaching Mitchell's quavering adolescent soprano to harmonize "Don't sit under the apple tree" by a mere two years. His junior year at Osprey High marked her first year of teaching. His maturity and her lack of it balanced the six years' difference in their ages.

They met at the first of what were to become annual Fourth of July picnics at Italo's. Italo walked the group—there were ten that year—on the short path from his home to the workshop, where he persuaded Mitchell to demonstrate his skill.

The young man blew a glass sphere and later presented it to Twyla. He had never seen such a fair-skinned woman. Her red hair shimmered like a halo in an old religious painting. At the beach she wore a hat and a jersey over her bathing suit and wrapped herself in thin blankets to prevent her skin from turning lobster-red.

No one ever knew whether curiosity or fate inspired Twyla to tell Mitchell she'd be pleased to learn glassblowing. In later years she herself said many times she had neither intent for romance nor talent for other than the diatonic scale.

The day after the picnic, Mitchell escorted Twyla to the shed beneath the tulip tree in his parents' backyard. There he had the lamp-working equipment he had used since he was nine to create glass vases, shells, and starfish. Twyla sat on a stool at the end of the asbestos-covered worktable, while Mitchell slipped a blue cobbler's apron over his head.

"Let me try," Twyla said, after watching him shape a small vase; it looked so easy. She chose a piece of glass tubing and Mitchell guided her through the steps.

"Hold it up. Up!" he said, as she turned the glass in the flame of a Bunsen-type burner. When the time was right she blew a large, uneven bubble, wincing when it burst into pieces.

She tried again and again until she managed to blow a fairly even sphere, but enough was enough. Patience was not one of her virtues, she had to admit, and from that time on she left the blowing of glass to Mitchell.

At noon they carried their lunch through the woods to the marsh. Tangles of briars lined the dense path and caught the hem of Twyla's seersucker skirt. Cobwebs spanned the trail and clung to Mitchell's light hair as he led the way.

"Watch for poison ivy," he warned. "Three shiny leaves."

Birds chirped frantically as the two emerged from the trees and moved down the embankment to the marsh. Mitchell held out his arm to halt Twyla's progress. There in the marsh grass walked a family of Canada geese, two full-grown and five medium-size goslings.

"This place is magical," Mitchell said, and at the sound of his voice the family loped off into one of the curving tidal creeks that cut like a maze through the cordgrass.

Mitchell led Twyla to a long, flat rock near the water's edge, and the geese, honking madly, rose up from the river and flew toward the sea.

"My rock," Mitchell said, and he offered it to her with a bow, as if it were the finest of sofas. They sat on the hunk of granite that glinted with specks of mica. Pale gray-green lichen grew on its sides. Tiny red bugs traversed the ups and downs of its contours, a fiddler-crab claw rested in a hollow.

The birds became quiet; the marsh grass, six feet tall, rustled like taffeta. At high tide, water crept up around the peat any which way, wherever it found a cup or a hollow. After some distance, the indefinite borders of the creeks met and broadened into the Blue Crab River.

As they ate Twyla's fried chicken and potato salad, they saw in the distance the metallic glint of the railroad bridge, the highest structure around. The one tower they could see stood tall and thin, like a soldier made from a giant erector set. Girders hung down either side of the tower like arms; a pointed hat topped with a ball of flaming mercury glistened in the sun.

Not a soul around until, lunch consumed, they were about to depart and saw, on the far side of the river, a rowboat moving slowly, silently, the figure rowing a black brushstroke against the blue, blue water.

Then back through the undergrowth: mosquitoes, dying foxglove, small freshwater stream. From that day on Mitchell and Twyla were inseparable.

Town gossip began with low murmurs and mumblings as the two were seen strolling about hand in hand. One day some folks observed them on the far side of the St. Barnabas Episcopal Church, kissing. Town gossip crescendoed; Twyla's status as new music teacher became shaky. Called into the superintendent's office and warned of the consequences of her behavior, Twyla applied for and secured a position teaching music in Plymouth. This appeased some and gossip leveled off as the couple continued to date throughout Mitchell's junior and senior years. Gossip crested once more at the engagement; climaxed with the marriage a week after Mitchell's high-school graduation; and, within a matter of years, faded.

By the time he was twenty-four, Mitchell created glassworks fine enough to be considered art. In 1952, Twyla beside him in the Chevy, they journeyed to a glassworks exhibition near Syracuse, New York. The two Bishops and every piece of glass Mitchell had blown in the past year—wrapped carefully and stashed in the backseat and trunk—were shattered to instantaneous extinction when the car went over the side of a mountainous road in the Berkshire fog. Damaris—just three—had remained behind with her grandparents and did not understand what they meant when they said she was an orphan.

[2]

Summer—1966

The day is warm and the village quiet. Unlike many Cape villages, North Osprey remains fairly isolated, pretty much unknown to the tourists who descend onto the sandy spit between May and October.

At one time Grover Cleveland owned a house nearby, overlooking the harbor and canal entrance, but despite this minor claim to fame, the village keeps a low profile. At its most bountiful the center boasts a post office, Queen's Department Store (a miniature Woolworth's), a one-room library, and two churches.

Damaris, now seventeen, stands on the sidewalk beneath the open window of Italo Benovucci's workshop, listening to the hum of the fans.

Since she'd been a child she'd searched for the why and how of her father in the craft Italo pursued; searched for a trace of Mitchell in the faint, shimmery lushness of molten glass turned solid.

By the time she was eight she'd just about become a fixture at the shop. Italo declared that if she was going to hang around she might as well be useful and he gave her odd chores to complete.

When Lucy Benovucci died last April, Italo promoted Damaris to work on the account books two days a week after school. They'd been neglected for some time, as Lucy had been ill since January and Italo left that sort of thing up to her, claiming he had no patience with bills.

Not that Damaris has much more. She'd rather hightail it out to the marsh. When she stands by the creeks, the air scented with lilac and honeysuckle, she envisions ancient Egypt. Why, she doesn't know, but when the dark green cordgrass grows tall, she wouldn't be surprised to find a reed basket with a baby inside, floating on the Blue Crab River.

She debates playing hooky, but a sense of duty overtakes her and she enters the brick building. A stranger sits on the bench beside the display cases in the salesroom; a man so dark he appears to be a shadow. Dark, glossy hair, black shirt with rolled-up sleeves, black cotton trousers.

"This is Logan Perth," Italo says. "I've hired him to assist you with the bookkeeping, organize the Christmas orders, maybe try a hand at some glasswork."

She barely has a chance to nod in the man's direction before Italo leads her into the new office, added last year.

"Not only a bookkeeper, but a painter," Italo says, as he gestures toward sheets of watercolor paper spread out on the desk. "A fine artist."

Neat, precise, the paintings look like old tapestries. Delicate, elaborate designs of flowers, birds, trees.

"They remind me of Lucy's work," Italo remarks.

Death must have glorified his wife's craft, Damaris thinks, as she regards the old man skeptically. Stenciling flowers on curtains and trays is mere puttering compared to these.

"Nah," Italo continues, more sensibly. "Much finer than Lucy's—may she not look down on us to hear—much finer."

Logan Perth has come from Maine in a beat-up Nova to settle the sale of land owned by his great-grandfather. As negotiations are difficult and extensive, he rents a room in Jose Santos's boardinghouse, takes the job with Italo.

"From the sign out front, I figured Jose to be a man," Logan says slowly to Damaris, pronouncing each word with care. "Spanish or Mexican. What a surprise to discover the name is 'Josie' and he's a she."

When he first speaks to Damaris in this laborious manner she thinks he's condescending, but she soon realizes this is his normal pattern of speech.

Throughout the summer Damaris and Logan pore over the books together, send bills and pay bills, organize Lucy's haphazard filing system.

While they work, Logan reveals bits and pieces of his life. He tells her he lives on a small island in Penobscot Bay, reachable only by boat. Like living in a land time forgot—electricity has not yet come to Perth Isle, telephones and hot running water are unknown.

As he speaks, he makes notations in the ledger. His hands are deeply veined, as if he is an old man, but he tells her he is twenty-seven. Only the necessity to complete the sale has drawn him away from home, for he's left his father behind, alone and ailing.

Slow as he is of speech, Logan is lightning in the blowing room, where Italo teaches him to gather the glowing orange glass from the furnace on a long, slender gathering iron.

They move quickly and efficiently from one step to the next in some sort of intuitive choreography. Logan carries the gather to the marner, a thick piece of flat steel mounted on a four-foot-high table, and rolls and shapes the gather against the steel.

Now Italo takes over, blows a bubble, then shapes the glass at the workbench. Steam rises from the wet wooden paddle he uses to lure the honeylike silica into form. Every now and again Italo carries the vessel to the oven for reheating, then reworks it and adds a stem, cutting the glass like taffy with his shears. He attaches the glass to a pontil, another long iron, and shapes the top. When Italo has finished, Logan sets the piece in the annealing oven to cool overnight.

In Logan, Damaris sees some shadow of her father, some rough echo of Mitchell's rhythm and craft. How can one person be so versatile? Logan's paintings and drawings are finely rendered and delicate, yet he is not delicate, for here he is, working alongside Italo, doing the work Damaris longs to do. "It's hot, tough, and demanding," Italo told her a few years ago when she asked to learn. "Very few women can bear the physical strain." At first upset by Italo's rejection, she later resolves to find her own way, though what that way is she has not yet discovered.

"How did you come to be an artist?" Damaris asks Logan late one night. Seated at the worktable, cluttered with thin bristled brushes, tubes of color, jars of water, Logan completes some finicky details on one of his paintings.

"I'm a craftsman," he replies, in an abrupt, distant manner.

Her face saddens at his tone. She knows this can't be true, knows somehow that such beauty coming from deep inside him surpasses craft.

"Will you teach me to paint sometime?" she asks, as she runs the soft bristles of a paintbrush against her cheek. "Grandmother says it's nearly impossible to teach me much of anything because I'm left-handed."

He looks at her then and she imagines he sees her sadness. Not simply the sadness at his distracted tone a moment ago, but the sadness of her life. Sees it without her having to speak.

"Perhaps someday," he tells her, his voice once again quiet and slow. But for now he claims the need to be alone and with gentle words asks her to leave.

Rather than going home, she lingers behind the shop, spys on Logan through the rear window as he hunches over the table in his serious way, doing his meticulous, womanly work.

The wait seems interminable, but only twenty minutes pass that night when the lights go out in the office and she tiptoes to the front of the building to follow Logan.

Some distance behind him she creeps along, hiding behind bushes and trees. At the end of the lane she risks discovery as she follows him across the only well-lit street in town. Does he have a secret girlfriend? She wonders.

In front of the St. Barnabas Episcopal Church he pauses to light a cigarette. She scoots behind a hedge and peers out.

Gone. Hurrying onto the sidewalk, she runs to where he once stood.

"What are you doing, wandering the streets at night?" Logan asks, as he comes around behind her.

She faces him and, in that moment, in the faint light of the faraway streetlamp, he appears beautiful; more wondrous than the marsh in the light of the full moon.

"I forgot to say good-night," she says.

He takes a step toward her. "I'll walk you home."

"No need." Hands before her palms up, she wards him off, backs away as if from the heat of the glory hole.

For a moment on the way home she thinks she hears him whisper to her in the dark, whisper her name, whisper good-bye, but the sound is that of a bird in its nest, settling down to sleep.

Italo Benovucci speaks of forgoing his annual Fourth of July picnic this year because of Lucy's death, but the work is out of his hands. His sisters from Boston arrive a week ahead of time to help prepare for the event. The women feel the picnic will do Italo good; what better time to be surrounded by family than when one is in mourning, the sisters say.

The day of the picnic, Damaris wears a new sundress with spaghetti straps, lemon yellow to match her hair. In front of her mirror she spins round, watches the full skirt billow.

"It's time you wore something on your legs," Grandmother says. She appears in the bedroom door and extracts a garter belt and pair of sheer stockings from a Queen's Department Store bag.

"It's too hot," the girl says, but she takes the belt, a blue belt with yellow daisies printed on the cloth and a tiny bow at the waist.

"I don't go anywhere without my stockings," the old woman says, still peering into the bag. "I meant to buy myself a pair of earrings."

Damaris lifts her skirt and hooks the belt.

"Under your pants, child," Grandmother says, as she gives up her search for the jewelry and folds the bag into a square.

Once Damaris fastens the belt properly, Grandmother demonstrates how to roll the stockings down and ease the foot in to avoid a run, which to Grandmother seems to be the biggest sin this side of lust.

Damaris attaches the stockings to the metal garters, then slips on her sandals. As she twirls once more in front of the mirror, the stockings swish like a flock of sparrows swooping in flight.

The Benovuccis's white-stucco house is unusual in this region of weathered shingles. Italo's father designed and built the house in Osprey and a number of others in the small Italian neighborhood under the shadow of the Sagamore Bridge.

By the time Damaris and her grandparents arrive, guests are scattered about on the lawn and gathered in clusters around the two long tables holding food and liquor.

Damaris crosses the yard to the summerhouse near a stand of birch trees. The long, wooden summerhouse swing creaks and rattles as she pumps her feet and watches the picnickers drift back and forth from sun to shade, from group to group. Someone sets up a croquet game and the balls click and thud. Damaris is about to claim the red mallet when Logan, in a blue shirt and khaki pants, separates from the gathering and heads toward her.

There seems something exotic about him. She imagines he might have business with olive trees and thyme-covered hillsides. He reminds her of Sunday School Bible illustrations of David, or Joseph of the coat of many colors.

"Have you been to these affairs before?" Logan asks, as he hands her a paper cup of punch.

"For years and years." Their fingers touch when she takes the drink.

"I'm not used to so many people." Logan sits on a wooden bench nearby. "We had one neighbor on the island who died when I was ten. His shack is deserted, the walls have fallen in, only the cellar is left."

She hardly hears his words. His face fascinates her. The movement of the muscles above his jaw as he speaks, the fleshiness beside his mouth. His nose is almost elegant, almost too pointy.

"How did you go to school?"

"In good weather my mother and I motored in *The Sea Whip* to nearby Windhaven Island. Once I was old enough, I took the boat myself, but winters are rough on the water and Mother kept me home. She tutored me and taught me to paint and draw. . . . Mostly I fished. My father earned his living fishing and he thought I'd follow him." He removes a pack of Camels from his pocket, shakes one loose, and offers it to her. "But I surprised him. I moved off the island for a time, lived on the mainland in Fairweather Harbor, studied bookkeeping."

Damaris places the cigarette between her lips. Dry. He removes another for himself. Unlit, it dangles from the corner of his mouth as he speaks.

"I wanted something more practical than painting, less rigorous than fishing, to turn to, though fishing's what I've done since returning to the island to care for my father."

He strikes a kitchen match against the sole of his shoe, holds the light toward Damaris. She inhales and coughs.

Logan laughs, shakes his head. "You don't smoke."

"Oh, yes, I do. But I gave it up for a time."

She moves forward, crosses her sweaty, itchy legs, longs to run barefoot. But it wouldn't be proper to remove her stockings here. As she squirms, the nylon catches on a splinter and tears.

"Grandmother'll skin me alive."

"Let's see," Logan says, laughing again.

Damaris jumps down and turns for him to examine the back of her leg. With one hand she lifts her hem, with the other she holds the cigarette away from herself, shoulder height, as Bette Davis does in the movies. When Logan touches the tear she jumps and almost burns his forehead.

"If I can repair nets, I can repair this." He withdraws the cigarette from her fingers, smokes it as they walk the few blocks to his room.

Hair like fine spun glass spills out of her ponytail. As she strides beside him, breathless, a longing fills her, a longing to follow him through the world as she'd followed him through the town, only a month ago.

A wide porch extends around the front and sides of the large yellow house with white trim topped by one of the few widow's walks in town. Jose's husband had bought the place in a good year for fishing but a bad year for real estate. Its size had provided the widow with an income for more than twenty years, not to mention the space to raise nine children. The children were grown now but they flocked to the boarding-house on the Fourth of July, their children in tow.

"Logan, Logan, come join us for a clam boil," Jose says, when Damaris and Logan enter her kitchen. Steam billows out of the huge graniteware pot on the stove. "Look. A Cape Verdean specialty. Clams, quahogs, mussels topped with *chouriço*. You know *chouriço?*"

"Perhaps later," Logan says politely.

"And you," Jose continues, not bothered by Logan's response, in fact dishing shellfish onto a plate. "You're the Bishop orphan, aren't you?"

Jose's voice is high, like a midget's. Damaris thinks she might be a midget, short as she is. "Pleased to meet you, Mrs. Santos," she says, and holds out her hand in greeting.

"Oh, Jose, Jose, please call me Jose. You know Jose?" she shouts, as if it strains her to speak. She places a plate piled high with sausage and shellfish in Damaris's outstretched hand.

"Now there's sweet bread, that's Portuguese bread. You know Portuguese? And potato and Jell-O salads outside on the table. Help yourself. Ask Horacio or Agnes for anything you can't find."

Encumbered with a steaming plate topped with two sweet rolls whether he wants it or not, Logan climbs the broad front staircase to his room and Damaris follows with glasses of iced tea. They spread the picnic on a table in front of the window.

The room is sparsely furnished. A dresser and a double bed with iron springs, a thin mattress and no spread, stand opposite the window. On one wall Logan has mounted five fishing rods evenly spaced like the lines in a musical staff.

"I love rubber," he says, when he notes her interest in his fishing gear. "Boots, that is. And canvas." He displays a canvas bag stuffed with lures and lines.

"Jose is funny," Damaris says, once they are seated. She laughs. "Why does she talk like that, repeating herself. You know, repeat?"

Logan explains that years ago an accident injured Jose's vocal cords and she thinks she's difficult to understand. Embarrassed by her insensitivity, Damaris determines to eat in silence.

When Logan leaves the room for butter in which to dip the clams, Damaris hurries to his bookcase near the bed, where she finds a dusty Bible, a brown, flaky mystery. On the bottom shelf lies a ringed sketchbook, the pages covered with designs in muted watercolors: grays, blues, and browns. The pictures seem to illustrate the inner regions of her own self, her loneliness splattered on the page. If only she could paint like this.

Footsteps. Caught with book in hand, she blushes. "When will you . . . when will you teach me to paint?" she asks with a stammer, as she awkwardly returns the book to the shelf.

Soon, he promises, soon, and suggests she purchase a sketchbook, pencils, and brushes in preparation.

After they've eaten, Logan turns his back while Damaris unfastens both stockings, rolls them down and off, glad to be rid of the itchy nylon. As he dabs varnish on the tear with a brush, she stands straight and rigid, her feet close together. At some future time he will stand close, he will guide her hand across the page, he will whisper advice in her ear. But for now she must hold herself in abeyance when she is near him, hide what she most desires. She gazes out the second-story window into the tops of the oaks and maples that surround the house and, out of the corner of her eye, observes Logan's chest rise and fall beneath his blue cotton shirt.

They return to the Benovuccis' picnic late in the evening, when the group walks, en masse, to reserve a spot for the fireworks on short, rocky Osprey Beach. Some wear bathing suits to take a dip beneath the stars in the warm, seaweedy water, protected from the open ocean by the bay.

The Fourth of July brings everyone together. Old men, with old women on their arms, carry folding canvas lawn chairs and Thermoses of tea or whiskey. Whole generations of families, a bit tipsy from a day's worth of wine and rich food, cover vacant spots on the sand like flocks of sandpipers. Children, excited by a late night out, run back and forth across the beach, giggling, shouting, playing tag, impatient for the show to begin.

As far from her grandparents as possible, Damaris reclines on a towel.

"Will you share?" Logan asks, and she moves aside and pats the space next to her. Sitting beside Logan in the darkness, their knees nearly touching, she fancies she smells tobacco and the faint odor of turpentine and fish.

"Have you ever been married?" she asks, as they watch the crowd.

"I almost married once, a weaver, but she moved to Canada. . . ."

His voice is drowned out by the first fireworks, snapping like popcorn, rumbling like thunder. Brilliant colors spread through the air: red, blue, and that bright, bright yellow, almost brighter than the stars. In the bay, each wave is a glistening eye catching the light, reflecting the explosions; tiny fireworks in the sea.

August. The week of the county fair. This is Italo's first year running a booth. At the workshop the large metal garage-type doors stand open. Logan unlatches the pickup tail gate and climbs into the truck bed. Italo and Damaris hand him the fragile boxes packed with glass.

"I don't know if it's worth the trouble," Italo said last week; Lucy had reserved their space months ago.

"No sense backing out now," Logan said, and offered to

work the stand with Damaris and relieve Italo of the chore.

Damaris sweats in her T-shirt and shorts. The fairgrounds in Marston's Mills, at one of the most inland points possible, steam and swelter. No hint of a breeze. The tires of the pickup stir the dust as they weave among the other trucks and head for the tent assigned to crafts.

They unload boxes, set up their wares. By two-thirty they are organized and Logan sets Damaris free to explore the fair until the official opening.

Food sizzles at the concession booths. The smell of fried dough, at first whiff tantalizing, soon becomes nauseating. Elvis, Fats Domino, and The Supremes blast over the loudspeakers. Georgio Correia, who has some sort of monopoly on rides, spins the empty Ferris wheel round and round to test the gears, bright lights flashing.

Past the house of horrors, past the ride that twirls you upside down in a basket, past dart games, past a tent swathed in deerskins with a sign beside the door announcing CARD READINGS—FUTURES TOLD. Past a woman on cushions eager to massage your feet, past cotton candy and french-fry booths, grease hanging in the air above them.

"Put your money on a color, win a monkey!" hollers a teenaged vendor. Damaris smiles, then backtracks to the deerskin tent.

The dirty skin covering the door makes her cringe. The old Wampanoag woman inside looks up, startled. A woven shawl lays on the floor beside a beaded headdress.

"I know I'm early. This is my only chance."

The woman dons her headdress, wraps the shawl around her, dims the kerosene lantern.

"Give me your watch."

Damaris hands the watch to her and when the crooked, brown fingers touch hers she yearns for her mother.

"Yes?"

"I might . . . I might be in love. . . ."

"Ah, and what would you know of love? So young. Once loved, a creature remains forever loved, though intensity ebbs and flows. Love is the medium through which your wisdom will come. The wisdom holds the power. One dollar."

Out on the grounds again, Damaris pushes the words into the corner of her thoughts. The woman hardly seems to belong to the noisy, smelly fair, so ethereal, so nonsensical is she.

The carnival noises fade as she approaches the animal tents: rabbits, sheep, chickens, goats. She holds out her hand for a calf to lick. His hot, rough tongue sends shivers up her neck and she remembers the sandwich of calf's tongue Grand-père once fed her and which she discarded when he wasn't looking.

On her return she buys fried dough and sausage and presents them to Logan for dinner.

"Delicious," he says, biting into the greasy sandwich. "This is one food I'll miss when I leave, this and *caldo verde*. Kale doesn't grow on the island."

Leave? Damaris hasn't seriously thought about his leaving, but there is no time to ruminate as people trickle in. By five-thirty a continuous flow of onlookers keeps her occupied protecting glass from curious fingers.

Logan and Damaris arrive at a smooth rhythm, joking and chatting between customers, as they work steadily, side by side, selling cup plates, inkwells, paperweights, and pitchers. He handles the cash; she wraps the glass in layers of tissue.

"How about going for a spin?" Logan asks one night, as soon as the fair closes. He leads her to the Ferris wheel, having bargained with Georgio Correia to stay open for one last ride, just for the two of them.

Damaris climbs into the metal cage and Logan squeezes in close beside her. There is no room to spread out. The door clicks shut, the music flourishes, and the cage tips slowly as the wheel begins to turn. "Sure is dark out tonight," she says, before she realizes her eyes are shut as tight as quahog shells. By the time she pries them open, they have traveled halfway to the top.

Logan laughs and puts his arm around her, much to her relief. She has never acclimated to heights, never had to on Cape Cod; the land is flat as a pancake. Flatlanders the natives are called by folks in other parts of the state.

They spin up and around in a full circle a number of times before she is aware of his knee and thigh pressing close, of his fingers warm against her arm. On the final revolution Georgio, a tiny fellow far below, stops the wheel at the top and the cage sways slightly as they pause, suspended in space. Logan whispers, "You okay?" And his breath tickles the fine hairs in her ear.

"Sure," she replies, and, envisioning them as lovers, she turns her face toward his, lips so close he might kiss her, but the moment is lost as the wheel jerks and they descend to the waiting Georgio.

By the last day of the fair they have sold much, broken little.

"Italo will be pleased," Logan says, as they stack boxes of unsold goods in the workshop late that night. When they finish, he produces a bottle of wine. They find paper cups in the bathroom and he waters down her portion. "Don't want to be accused of contributing to the delinquency of a minor."

"I'm nearly a major." She stands straight to look more mature.

"To Italo," Logan says, and raises his cup to touch hers in a toast.

"To the summer," she adds.

"The county fair."

"And the Ferris-wheel ride." How near he had been, how warm his thigh had been against hers.

"To *chouriço* and dough fried."

"You're a poet and don't know it . . ." she begins.

Laughing, they complete in unison, ". . . but your legs show it, they're long fellows." As they laugh they come together for a moment, and their arms brush as Damaris stumbles in her awkwardness. She rights herself, steps away, though she'd rather step forward, hide in the cool, dark shadow of his form.

"I'm hungry," she says. "Starved." She opens the door of the apartment-sized refrigerator, finds apples, a chunk of moldy cheddar. With a knife used for slicing string from packages, she pares off the mold. There is enough good cheese to form a small mound of golden steps on a paper towel. Logan slices the apples into half-moon eighths and in a desk drawer they find a box of Ritz crackers, slightly soggy but edible.

They spread the feast in the center of an old rag rug Lucy had made. Logan stretches out lengthwise and Damaris sits primly cross-legged some distance away, leans against the cool wood of the desk. A cracker, a square of cheese, a slice of apple; how delicious, almost gourmet. This is how life should be, she thinks as she sips the forbidden wine.

"I regret you've never shown me the marsh you love."

"It's lovely in October."

"October, yes . . . well . . ."

This is one food I'll miss when I leave. . . . The words rise in her memory and now she's no longer hungry but slightly dizzy from the heat, the wine.

"Let's go tonight," she suggests.

"Too dark."

"There's a flashlight in here somewhere in case the electricity goes out." They search the office and find two. The batteries are old, the light dim, but Logan rolls up the rug and Damaris packs the viands in a sack and off they go into the silent North Osprey morning.

Mitchell's path to the marsh is well worn these days, the land traversed by Boy Scouts and hunters, by bird watchers and teenagers gathering for beer parties. Damaris leads the way she knows by heart; the faint light illuminates roots and branches to avoid. She has never been to the marsh this early in the morning.

Logan spreads the rug over the dusty miller and sandwort. Once settled, he pours Damaris more wine. Straight. The full moon lights the morning, the stars glisten overhead.

"This place makes me homesick," he says.

"Do you have a marsh?"

"It's more the wet peace, the fine mist."

"Are you often homesick?" she asks, and holds her breath. Here it comes, leaving, leaving.

"Father writes that he can't care for himself alone any longer."

"How sad to be old and alone," she says, then feels the words are insensitive, inadequate.

"I'll return soon. I must."

"No . . ." she shouts, or it sounds like a shout to her ears. He can't leave. He's her friend. He's going to teach her to paint. "No doubt it's best," she says, and sips her wine, embarrassed by her outburst.

"Got a cigarette?"

"I've started you on a bad habit." He moves beside her then, but rather than take out his Camels, he touches her hair lightly. "Frizzy from the mist," he says.

He puts his arm around her shoulder and despite her longing she flinches at the touch, spills wine on his pants. He sops up the liquid with a handkerchief.

"As Grandmother tells it, my parents fell in love here, on this very spot."

"It certainly is romantic," he says, drawing her close.

And here they are again, knee to knee, thigh to thigh. She lifts her face to his once again, as on the Ferris wheel. She will seal their friendship with love, stake her claim with love.

I'm so lonely, she thinks, but all she says is, "I'll miss you."

He takes her hand, kisses the skin above her knuckles, kisses her fingers one by one.

The moon pales, the sun is about to rise, when she returns home, crawls in her bedroom window so as not to awaken the elders.

In bed, she wonders if he will stay now or, if he must leave, take her with him to Maine. She removes her watch and holds it as the old Wampanoag woman had, straining her vision into the future, but she sees only herself, lying on the rug with Logan, loving him on the damp marsh peat, the dark, narrow shape of the railroad bridge towering still and somber above them.

"What's a seven-letter word for 'without a hitch'?" Damaris asks her grandfather three months later. They are working together on a crossword puzzle in the kitchen. Pere sits in his rocker by the stove, hunched over the dictionary on his lap.

"Well, now, let's see," he says.

Damaris watches him thumb through the pages. She hesitates, breathes deeply. She dreads this revelation, anticipates the disruption the announcement will cause. Gone is any faint chance for winning applause; it is censure she will now incur. "I'm pregnant," she says.

Pere looks up slowly, peers at her for a moment, his face uncertain. "That the solution, or that a statement of fact?"

" 'Pregnant' is an eight-letter word, not seven."

"Who's to blame?" Pere says, as he rocks forward in his chair.

Her fingers tighten around her pencil.

Pere's face turns red, his jaw clenches. "Answer me," he says, as he rises from the chair, slams the dictionary before her on the table.

"He's gone."

One cold morning in early September she saw Logan off in the beat-up Nova. Rubber boots, jackets, tackle boxes, and clothes crowded the backseat. A framed print of fish leaping from the water—"breaking," as he called it—rested on top.

Logan climbed into the car, opened the window, and leaned out. "You've been a good friend," he said.

Good friend. Good friends don't part this way. Good friends move along together. She had no suitcase, had never traveled, never ventured beyond Cape Cod, but hidden in the bushes was her laundry bag stuffed with clothes, her new sketchbook still blank, her pencils unsharpened. If he'd said come along, she'd have hopped into the car, mailed a note to her grandparents later. "Take . . ." she began, then faltered. *Me along,* she wanted to say, but she was too proud to impose herself on him. He must want her to come, ask of his own free will without prompting from her. "Take care."

Instead of an invitation, he handed her a sheet of paper covered with an intricate design: the curves of shrimp, sleek lines of eels, brown, blue, and gray fish, glittering creatures breaking and swimming in pairs. A piece of him to hold in her hand.

"I'll write," he promised, and he waved, waved as her parents had waved so many years before, never to return. And the gold car drove away, the rods on top whirring in the wind.

Pere turns Damaris's head to one side, raises his hand as if to slap her, but he barely skims her cheek.

"I remember when you sat in that rocker and your feet wouldn't touch the floor." He sighs and turns away.

"You held the music box in your lap and rocked and listened for hours, singing the tune. What was it?"

" 'Frère Jacques.' "

"Well . . . no more of that." He curses and calls, "Claire," as he stomps down the hall to Grandmother's room.

Damaris returns to the puzzle, but the letters blur, the black lines merge. She blinks, holds the newsprint sheet near her eyes. The page quivers and she lets the thin booklet flutter to the table, drops the pencil.

Grandmother enters the kitchen swiftly in her pink chenille bathrobe and black, flowered slippers with holes in the toes. Pere follows.

"We want to talk to him," Grandmother says. They stand before Damaris like guardians to the garden of the righteous, but Damaris sees the dismay in their eyes.

"I don't know where he is." As Damaris tells this lie, she straightens her back, sits firm and rigid. Logan had written out his address: in care of Mrs. Twine, Haven Inn, Wind-haven Island. "I'll write," he had said. For three months she's checked the mailbox daily. Not a word yet, though she's certain he'll write, certain he'll keep his promise.

"*Two boys* wouldn't be as much trouble as you," Pere says.

Thump. His fist thuds against the table. The salt shaker wobbles.

"Fourteen years we've cared for her and this is the thanks we get," he says, as he gestures widely, addresses some audience beyond the kitchen, the town of Osprey, perhaps.

"We want to know who the father is," Grandmother says firmly.

"Some irresponsible hoodlum, no doubt. Some nefarious character . . ."

"Franklin, please," Grandmother says. The old man trembles slightly and his voice winds down like a music box at the end of its play.

Damaris isn't sure who irritates Grandmother more, her grandchild or her husband.

"I'm sure once you've had time to think it over you'll tell us. It's for your own good," the old woman says, and, linking her arm through Grand-pere's, they depart.

The next morning as Damaris prepares her lunch for school, Grand-pere enters the kitchen.

"Been awake half the night," he says. "It's that Logan fellow. He's the one I've seen you with, never any high-school boys."

She spreads jelly on the peanut butter. "What difference does it make?"

"It's his duty to marry you. Taking advantage of a child." The old man paces back and forth; the blue-and-gray linoleum crackles beneath his boots.

"I'm not a child." She defends herself, but the words choke back in her throat. She is seized with a great turmoil in her stomach and intestines; morning sickness.

Grand-pere peers at her as if to determine how old she *is*. "Does this Logan know about the baby?"

"You're the only one I've told," Damaris replies, as she wraps the sandwich in waxed paper and tucks it into the brown bag. She will not write first, will not use the baby as leverage into Logan's heart.

"I'll find this Logan. I'll find him through Italo."

"Stubborn old man," Damaris says, and after picking up her books she opens the back door.

"I'll write to him myself!" Grand-pere shouts after her, when she is halfway down the sidewalk.

This is her problem. Why can't he leave it be? By the time Damaris reaches Main Street she determines to skip her first class and heads for the workshop. Grand-pere won't be the one to reveal her secret. If anyone tells Logan it will be herself—once he proves his love with a letter. In the office, she flips through the small metal file box, extracts the card with Logan's address, and tears it into pieces.

Grandmother sips a spoonful of quahog chowder. Her cheeks sag into jowls that tremble as she tentatively chews the tough bivalves with her loose lower dentures. She jumps up from the table to retrieve the forgotten butter, downs a bite of corn muffin, and leaps up again, returning with beach-plum jam.

Grandmother's been forgetting things more often lately, Damaris thinks. Must be old age.

Grand-pere lacks his usual irritation with his wife's forgetfulness. As he devours his soup and three muffins, his head bends over the food in total concentration; his long, thick-fingered hand circles the soup bowl. Tufts of white hairs like tiny, fluffy feathers cover his fingers. He eats noisily, sighing with the goodness of the food.

"I'm writing a paper on the cranberry industry for social studies. I'd like to interview you, Grand-pere. You worked the bogs, didn't you?" Damaris asks, to break the silence. No one has spoken a word since Grandmother announced dinner.

"Please pass the pickles," Grand-pere says, and dinner continues in strained silence.

Grandmother ladles out seconds on soup. Damaris breaks open a corn muffin, spreads it with butter, and inquires after Grand-pere's rheumatism. He merely glares at her, turns to Grandmother, and says, "Good chowder."

"I'll need money for a layette," the girl says, thinking this will rouse the old man. Grandmother slides to the edge of her chair, ready to arbitrate, but Pere merely says, "Didn't you say apple pie for dessert?" And the old woman jumps up once again.

"Apple pie," Pere says. "There's an irony here, Claire."

"Irony?" Claire repeats, as she slices the pie.

"We're reversing the order according to Genesis: sin first, apples second."

"That is ridiculous," Damaris says, dropping her unfinished muffin onto her plate. "I'll be studying in my room."

"Won't you have a piece of pie? You're eating for two now," Grandmother begins, but Damaris is down the hall and into her room before the old woman can finish.

The dissection of frog's innards and the discussion of Falstaff's antics loom dreary and impossible the next morning. The day is overcast, but warm. With her school books hidden in the shed, Damaris heads for the beach.

At the end of the driveway, she pauses. The mailbox opens with a shiver and a hollow sound, then quivers on its wooden pedestal when she slams the door on its emptiness.

Famished, she devours her tuna sandwich by the time she reaches the water. Eating for two. She munches the chips and Oreo cookies, crumples the bag.

The beach is damp and deserted. Pebbles clack as waves wash over them. A lone gull pecks at the remains of a fish, then flies off as Damaris combs the beach for water worn shards of glass. A piece here, a piece there, a lifetime of gathering renders but four and a half quart jars full, and those are mostly white and green with a smattering of blue. Ruby is what she longs for. When the light shines through the jars arranged on her window ledge the broken chips are transformed into a humble sort of stained-glass effect. She finds two greens and a brown before the light rain falls at noon.

She wanders along the road toward home, thinking to hide in the shed until school lets out, but she pauses by the yellow boardinghouse. The rain falls harder now. Taking shelter on the back porch, she sits among stacks of clay pots that held last summer's geraniums and lawn furniture covered in plastic, but the open porch affords little protection.

"I thought I saw a body out there," Jose says. Her broad, molasses-colored face peers out from behind the storm door. "What are you doing in that rain?"

"Just waiting out the storm."

"You'll catch your death. Now come on in for a cup of tea."

"I don't want to be a bother."

"You get on in here. Don't have to fetch you, do I?"

Damaris enters the kitchen, which is warm with the smell of yeast.

"Just fixing some bread and jag for the boarders' dinner. You know jag?"

Damaris shakes her head no as she sits at the round kitchen table.

"Rice and peas is how I make it, though some use the lima bean. How about a taste?"

"Well, I don't know. . . . I . . . ."

"Here," Jose says, setting a bowl and spoon before Damaris. "Expand your world." She pours two cups of tea and pulls up a chair opposite the girl.

"It's delicious," Damaris says.

"Nothing better when you're down than a bowl of jag."

"I'm not down," Damaris says. She turns to her drink, holds up her dripping tea bag.

"I always forget. Here you go." Jose scoots a saucer across the table. "I'd introduce you to my crew of boarders, but they nap after lunch. More like an old-folks home than a boardinghouse."

Damaris scrapes out the last of the rice with her spoon.

"Nice to hear a quick step on the stair. I did appreciate that young friend of yours, Logan Perth."

Damaris looks up sharply at the older woman, but Jose is busy stirring a spoonful of honey into her tea.

"You hear from that fella since he left?"

He will write. He promised! The words almost spill out as

she leaps to his defense. Surprised by the vehemence of her thoughts, she looks down. In her teacup float small leaves of tea, escaped from the bag. As the Wampanoag woman read the warmth of her watch, Damaris reads the tea leaves for an answer. If she waits long enough, they say, he will miss her, he will get in touch, a letter will come, proof of his caring.

"No need to hide your face in that teacup," Jose says, as she clears the table. "Never mind me, I'm just a nosy old lady who needs to get a move on. Going shopping with one of my girls."

"You sure do have a lot of kids."

"Yep. Quite a parcel."

"Were you scared the first time?"

"Scared. Girl, I was but fifteen. Here we were, my future husband and me, fixing to leave Fogo and head for New Bedford, when I come up pregnant. It didn't go over big, pardon the pun. But scared . . . well, let's see . . . I was excited . . . 'course, that was 'cause of the sea voyage ahead . . . hard to recall back that far . . . but, yes, I guess I was scared. Leaving my mama behind . . . heading off with my man and little Horacio tucked in my pouch. And me only speaking Crioulo."

"You were some adventuress." Damaris has heard of Fogo from kids at school. One of the islands of Cape Verde, off the coast of Africa.

"But it turned out fine in the end. Don't know where I'd be without my family."

"I wish I was part of your family," Damaris says, certain a mother like Jose would take her problem in stride.

"And wouldn't *that* be grist for the gossip mill."

Several days later, Damaris returns from school and enters the pantry for an apple. Grandmother perches on a long-legged wooden chair, a knife and hubbard squash before her on the cutting board.

"Take a seat, child," she says.

Damaris removes a stack of folded dish towels from the step stool and sits; her heels rest on the lowest rung.

Grandmother looks out the small window. "There he is, working hard as ever. I tell him he'll die before me the way he pushes himself. What would I do? I can't even balance a checkbook."

"No sense getting upset ahead of time," Damaris says.

Grandmother sighs. "I'm too old to change now. Stuck with who I am, good, bad, or indifferent."

"No one would ever consider you bad."

"Ah, well," Grandmother says, her left eye tearing. A linen handkerchief with a green tatted border appears out of the older woman's pocket and she wipes away the moisture. "Those eye drops affect these old eyes something awful."

No soothing words occur to Damaris. Wishing to offer some comfort, she pats her grandmother's broad, pale knee protruding from beneath the flowered hem of her housedress.

"Sometimes I just don't understand that man. . . . There wasn't anyone on earth more pleased with a grandchild than Franklin was with you."

Damaris glances out the window. Grand-pere leans against the tree, wipes his neck with a green bandanna.

"When he held you in his arms he seemed to let go his stubborn grudge against your father. . . ."

This is old hat to Damaris, this story of Pere's anger with Mitchell: how Pere forbade him to date her mother, how Mitchell rebelled, how Pere threatened to kick him out, how Grandmother hoodwinked Pere into talking with Reverend Thomas from the Episcopal Church, and how the Reverend somehow turned things around. Pere didn't banish Mitchell, but he didn't speak to him, either, not for months.

"He always did care for you something special. Remember the way you . . . did I already tell you this?" Grandmother asks, looking disoriented for a moment. Damaris shakes her head no.

"Well, you loved to play cowboys and Indians. You were jealous of Mary Jane Whitcomb's store-bought hobbyhorse, so Franklin carved you one himself, a funny horse's head on a stick."

Damaris nods and pictures the hobbyhorse pushed into the back of her closet, awaiting a child's touch once more.

"I'm bringing this up because, you see . . . well . . . if you won't contact the father, Franklin's determined to send you to a home."

"I've got a home," she says, a bit bewildered.

"One in Boston. For unwed mothers."

Now Damaris's eyes fill with tears. How can it enter their heads to do that? She recalls suddenly the girl at school, Maisey Williams. How one day she was there and the next gone completely. Not at school, not in the village. Murmurs and whispers: ". . . the sort who goes all the way . . . trip to the city . . . put up for adoption . . ." The girl had reappeared half a year later and quietly resumed her studies at night school.

"I have asked him," Grandmother continues, "to consult with someone again. Of course, Reverend Thomas passed away, but there's a new minister, younger, more modern in outlook. But Père is adamant this time. I am sorry, dear," she concludes, and places her cold, thin fingers against Damaris's cheek.

Damaris hesitates, uncertain if Grandmother has more to say. But the old woman sighs, grasps the knife, and, after several attempts, slices through the hard rind of the squash, then scrapes the seeds and stringy pulp out with her fingers.

"Why won't you be reasonable?" Damaris asks Pere, in a loud voice, but her resolve to be strong diminishes as the old man continues his work, breaking twigs and laths into small pieces for the stove, his back turned toward her.

Dejected, the girl wanders to the shed, now a storehouse for the lawnmower, tools, and rubble Grand-pere has saved over the years. She kicks the door open and steps inside.

Shelves hold dusty boxes of glass tubes. On top of the asbestos-covered table an old Bunsen-style burner rests on its side between clippers and gardening gloves. In a drawer she finds jacks and a red, rubber ball. The ball plops as it hits the cement floor.

The room fills her with a sense of loneliness. A small flicker of doubt rises on her certainty, like the soft down of moss on a shady lawn. How will she handle this alone? What will happen to her? Perhaps she should contact Logan.

Grand-pere appears in the door. "Pride goeth before a fall."

"I wonder," Damaris says, as if out of a dream, as if she hadn't even heard him, "what my father would have said to your wanting me to leave." Things would be different if he were alive; he would help her, she knows.

"Have I said anything about leaving?" Pere asks, entering the shed.

She remains silent, taps the red ball with her sneaker; it rolls against the old man's worn leather workboot.

"That woman talks too much."

"Do you think he'd have sent me away?"

Grand-pere stares at her for some time. He rumples his long, white hair, which he refuses to allow any barber to touch, though Grandmother gets her hands on it now and then.

"Well, I think he . . ." Damaris pushes on, but before she can continue her grandfather interrupts.

"We won't be shamed," he says firmly, his face flushed.

"But my father—"

"No bastard in my house."

"Your great-grandchild?"

"You must take responsibility for what you have done."

"I *am* responsible."

"You will go to Boston, put the child up for adoption," he says, his voice loud.

"You have no right—"

"In my house, the rights are mine."

"What's a nine-letter word for 'stubborn'? *Grand-pere,* that's what."

The old man grasps her by the shoulders and shakes her. For an instant she imagines he might carry her off as he'd done when she was a child, but she is not a child and she twists out of his grip.

"You will not talk to me that way. You're grounded," he says, as he moves toward the exit. "For the rest of your life." He leaves, slamming the shed door behind him.

Later that afternoon, Damaris sits on the living room couch awaiting dinner. She feels restless, anxious. Pere dials the phone in the kitchen, asks for a Mrs. Hutchinson.

"On another line?" he asks. "It's urgent. I must speak with her today. . . . Yes, I'll be home."

But Mrs. Hutchinson doesn't return the call until nearly dinner time the next afternoon. Damaris cracks her bedroom door to listen.

"Seventeen," Grand-pere tells the woman. "I don't know how long . . ."

That's all Damaris hears before she shuts and locks her door. A hard knot of resistance rises in her bones as she determines to keep the baby. The child will be hers, her companion, her friend. Someone to hold and care for. Someone who won't leave.

Once again she stuffs her laundry bag with the contents of her drawers, her music box, Logan's drawing. She spoke with

Jose that afternoon, just in case. Logan's room is still vacant, the rent reduced in exchange for cleaning and cooking. "Anytime, anytime," Jose said, asking no questions.

Damaris has a small savings account from her job with Italo; she won't think beyond these meager assurances. For the rest, it's as if . . . as if she is on an overgrown path on the marsh, forcing her way through the cordgrass and cattails, the horizon her guide, hope the support to keep her from sinking into the soggy peat.

There is a knock; the latch clatters.

"Unlock the door," Grand-pere says, and when Damaris makes no response he pounds harder. "Claire, Claire, see if you can talk some sense into this girl."

When Grandmother's soft soprano joins his baritone, Damaris opens the window, tosses out her parcel, and climbs over the sill onto the brittle grass below.

Later, at Jose's insistence, Damaris telephones home so they won't worry. She fears Pere may come after her, but he "washes his hands of the affair," Grandmother relays.

Then Pere picks up the extension and tells her, "Never cross my threshold again. The crossing of thresholds . . . that's reserved for brides."

[4]

On her first night in the room at Jose's, Damaris tacks Logan's drawing to the wall at the foot of her bed. She folds her underwear neatly into the dresser he used, sniffs in the drawers, in the closet where he hung his black chinos and suit, certain the faint odors of turpentine and fish permeate the closed-in spaces.

She places her sketchbook, the pages as white as Jose's sheets, on the bottom shelf of the bookcase as he had. *He was going to teach her to paint.*

She peers under the mattress and in the cupboards for something forgotten, combs the cushions for a lure, a match. Nothing. Jose's thorough cleaning.

That night she lies awake in the bed Logan had dreamed in. Since she'd been three she'd slept within the farmhouse walls and before that with her parents. The small flicker of doubt she felt in the shed flares once more and she wonders again if she should write to Logan. "Pride goeth before a fall," Grand-pere said. Is it pride that holds her back? As if to write first is a giving up, a giving in, an admission of weakness.

No, she will not be the first.

She traces a pattern along the headboard he'd rested against. Oils from his hair made the wood shiny. On her fingers she sniffs the fragrance of Murphy Oil Soap. Jose again, wiping out the odors of times past.

Several weeks after she moves to Jose's she drops out of school, quits her job at Italo's. Afternoons she helps Jose prepare the evening meal for the four other boarders.

"I can't cook for beans," she tells the diminutive woman at her elbow.

"Beans," Jose says, her high voice somewhat shrill. "That's what I'll teach you to cook." And she proceeds to instruct Damaris step by step.

"Now, *caldo verde,* kale soup, we'll make tonight," she says, as she removes a mass of rubbery green leaves from the vegetable bin and instructs Damaris to wash them like spinach. "I been working while you daydream. We got kidney beans cooked up fresh in this pot."

Jose clangs the lid off to give Damaris a peek, then clangs it back on.

"Now for the spuds."

She slams the potatoes onto the cutting board and hands Damaris the peeler.

"Peel and cube. Then we got linguiça and *chouriço*. I'll slice the sausage."

Jose drags a high, metal kitchen stool to the cutting board and sits beside Damaris.

"Am I glad you're here for Thanksgiving. Need all the help I can get. You are here for Thanksgiving?" She eyes Damaris inquisitively, raising her eyebrows and lowering her voice.

"As far as I know." The boardinghouse is not far from the old farm, but Grand-pere still forbids her to return. If he answers when she telephones, he simply hands the receiver to Grandmother without a word.

"Give me a few weeks," Grandmother tells her. "I know some secrets. I'll get around him. He'll change his mind," but the secrets must not hold any power, for so far he has not relented.

As soon as Damaris cubes the potatoes, Jose scoops them into the bean pot and hands her two large onions.

"Chop, please."

Damaris slices the pungent bulb into rounds.

"Wait, wait, wait," Jose says, and she demonstrates the proper way to chop onions. "Score down and across, then slice. Now, you try."

Tears form as Damaris cuts into the second onion. She runs to the sink and splashes cold water on her eyes as Grandmother taught her, but after she dries with a paper towel, tears come still and in a moment she is crying steadily, hiding her face from Jose with the towel. Before she knows it, Jose's arm is around her.

"What's the matter, child? I know something's wrong, but I don't like to pry."

"Just onions," Damaris says, not wanting to burden the older woman with her troubles. "Onions do this to me."

Later that afternoon, Damaris stacks dishes and soup bowls onto the oval dining room table.

"And how are we today?" asks Connie Grouse, a large woman with strands of hair from a blond-gray topknot perpetually dangling in her eyes. She squints over her tatting as she awaits dinner. Each night she arrives fifteen minutes early to ensure herself the same seat. She needn't worry. The others are equally adamant about retaining their usual places.

Second seated is generally Manuel Brito, an elderly gentleman somehow related to Jose.

"I am here against my will," he whispered to Damaris, soon after her arrival. "They dragged me out of my home when Mama Brito passed away. Forty years in a beautiful home, oh, so sad, so sad."

"It was the boardinghouse or a nursing home," Jose told Damaris, when the old man went on and on about his involuntary incarceration. According to Jose his house was a shack, with no heat except a kerosene stove.

Last down is Josiah Walters, at fifty or so the youngest of the crew, with speckled gray hair and a tic in his left eye so he appears to wink occasionally. The fourth roomer, Miss Winifred Cabot, aged eighty-five by the last count, dines in her room. The old woman's a bit of a hermit; can't tolerate anyone but Jose.

Damaris sets the blue-porcelain soup tureen in the center of the table and begins to serve.

"Does the soup contain meat?" Josiah, a vegetarian, inquires, and Damaris ladles him a portion minus sausage.

Jose enters with a basket of hot, sweet rolls.

"*Magnífico!*" Manuel Brito says.

The soup evokes positive comments. "Damaris's doing," Jose admits. "In fact, let's give her a hand." And she stands and claps and the others follow suit and won't cease until Damaris, blushing, rises and takes a bow.

After Damaris quits school, days seem vast and empty. Now and then, she opens her sketchbook and with a soft pencil attempts to render an orange or to capture the intricate patterns of the branches outside her window, but the sketches look like nothing she's ever seen, patches of lead smeared across the page.

Most often she fills the time by walking. On a warm day she might walk to the marsh. The salt-sogged grasses and gray, sandy mud smell of stagnation; the November wind is cold; the trees bare and the vegetation sparse. One afternoon she strolls behind Italo's workshop, spies through the rear window. Now it's Italo working at the table, never the dark man with the brush in his hand.

But usually she walks through the village, stopping in the church thrift store to search for baby clothes, sometimes spending nearly an hour rifling through piles of musty boots, old pocketbooks, gloves, kitchen utensils.

One day she finds a wicker baby carriage with large, heavy wheels. Magazines fall to the floor as she drags the yellowed carriage out of hiding from behind the library table stacked with books.

"An English carriage, a good sturdy beast," says the woman working the shop that day.

Damaris lifts the cushion padding the bottom.

"How much?"

The woman places her hand on Damaris's arm. "You'll need something like this when that one comes along, won't you?" She smiles and nods at Damaris's waist.

Small town. Can't keep a secret. "I haven't much money."

"Tag says thirty dollars. Seems steep, but I don't do the pricing. Maybe it'll go down after a time."

Can't keep a secret. The houses and sidewalks seem to hum with the sound of town gossip: When is it due? Who is the father, who? The faces she passes on her walks appear full of censure: *Shame on you for bringing disgrace to your grandfather. Shame. And after he spent his retirement years raising you. What kind of thanks is this? Ungrateful, ungrateful, ungrateful.* The words murmur and sweep through the air, as dry leaves rustle and twirl in a gust of wind.

She takes to walking after dark, when no one can see her, walking past the weather-beaten farm. She stands on the roadside by the oak tree, peers through windows into the lighted rooms.

Once Pere's shadow moves against the curtain, she leaves.

Unforgiving old man! She'll show him she can be a good mother, her child a blessing with or without a father. The baby kicks and rumbles inside her and the cold stings her hands as she returns to Logan's room.

On a snowy afternoon in mid-January, Damaris dry-mops the upstairs hall outside Miss Winifred's door. With the cold weather, she's given up her walks and stays inside, helping with chores and working crossword puzzles, though they're not as much fun alone. A vacuum would be more efficient, Damaris thinks, as she pushes wads of dust and bits of sand from one spot to another. Jose insists the hardwood floors be done this way.

Damaris sighs, and then, not wanting to slip into misery, so easily slipped into these days, she sings, "Frère Jacques, Frère Jacques, dormez-vous, dormez . . ."

"Is that you, Jose?" a voice shrieks from behind the closed door, interrupting the slightly off-tune rendition.

"Jose's shopping."

Silence. Damaris mops again, humming this time, but above her hum she hears a thump and thud from Miss Winifred's room.

"Are you all right?" Damaris asks through the closed door. Silence once more. She is about to turn the handle when the door cracks open, a face appears. Pale, pale white with tiny blue eyes shining; hair dry and sticking out above a slightly balding skull. No teeth.

"You the maid?" the old woman asks.

"I live here. Damaris," the girl says, and holds out her hand in greeting. The woman grasps Damaris's hand with cold fingers, her skin so thin the enlarged blue veins bulge clearly beneath.

"Come in, darlin'," Miss Winifred says, and she draws the girl toward her into a room so hot Damaris can barely breathe.

The elderly woman, smelling faintly of roses and dressed in white-flannel long johns, toddles toward her bed and climbs in.

"Adjust my pillows for me, darlin', won't you, now?"

Damaris straightens the tangle of pillows and blankets.

"There. That's fine. Now, get me my bed jacket. On top of the radiator. . . . No? Try the wicker rocker."

The room is a catastrophe. How can Jose, fanatical as she is about cleanliness, allow Miss Winifred to pile clothes, books, knitted afghans, and shoe box after shoe box of typewritten pages about the room this way? Dust catchers for sure. She helps Miss Winifred into the pink, somewhat grimy bed jacket.

"Thank you. Now, set that chair over here beside me. You're the maid, you said?"

Damaris explains once again.

"I see you got yourself in trouble. Well, never mind, darlin'. These things happen. Have been happening since man first gazed on woman in all her resplendent independence and beauty and determined to possess the beauty and repress the independence. Or, put another way, man took a gander at woman and longed to goose her." She laughs. "As they said in my day, 'keep 'em barefoot and pregnant.' "

At this she laughs again for some length of time until the laugh becomes inverted and she gasps for air.

"My tincture," she whispers, pointing to the bedside stand.

Damaris finds a small, brown bottle labeled "Lobelia Tincture—one teaspoon every hour during paroxysm." She hands the bottle to Miss Winifred, who swallows a spoonful with a glass of water and soon regains her equilibrium.

"And where's the perpetrator of this disaster?"

"Gone . . . I mean to say, he doesn't—"

"Doesn't know? Off the hook, as usual in these matters."

Logan. Already Damaris has forgotten what he looks like, remembers only yards and yards of fishing line, the way his fingers twirled the blowpipe laden with glass, the beauty of the paintings scattered on Italo's desk, the warmth of his touch. . . .

"Our arms touch," Miss Winifred says loudly, startling Damaris. "Our arms touch briefly—as we trek the long path—through scrub pine and oak."

"Pardon?"

"See those boxes?" Miss Winifred says, pointing to the far side of the room. "My life's work. Poems. Mostly unpublished."

"Like Emily Dickinson?" Damaris asks.

"Ah. You know poetry, then?"

"Oh, not really . . ." Damaris begins, but the woman continues.

"Maybe you'd like to read some. Not like Dickinson, not at all." She sighs. "I'm hungry."

"Shall I bring you a tray?"

"Can you poach an egg? That is the question."

"I've poached eggs for Grand-pere and he never complained."

"Grand-pere?"

"Franklin Bishop, my grandfather."

At this the old woman laughs so raucously Damaris thinks she'll need her tincture again, but she regains her breath in time.

"Do you know him?"

"Just bring me my poached egg. Toast on the side, with a good thick dab of Jose's rose-hip jam. And I thank you."

From that day on, Miss Cabot asks for Damaris and before long Jose turns over the care of the aged woman to the girl, including the sum of money the Cabot relations pay beyond the rent for her care.

Damaris assists the elderly woman with a shampoo at the

sink and remains by her side as she lowers herself slowly into the tub, for she fears slipping.

Miss Winifred's closet is full of old rayon and silk clothes and Damaris encourages her to dress. After a time the anti-quarian acquiesces. Several days a week she wears a dress under her bed jacket and over her long johns, though she never will exchange socks for hose or slippers for shoes.

"You sure have a way with that stubborn old woman," Jose says. "Try to get her downstairs for dinner."

But no powers of persuasion, no promise of éclairs or bawdy jokes, can lure her out of seclusion.

On the last day of January, Damaris balances a tray of dirty breakfast dishes against her hip with one hand and closes Miss Winifred's door with the other. With the money she's paid for Miss Winifred's care, Damaris makes small pur-chases: a dozen diapers, a bottle of baby oil, a box of safety pins, and a pacifier, until she accumulates the items that are of absolute necessity.

As Jose says when Damaris worries over preparations for the child, they will make do. "Make do" doesn't sound good enough to Damaris, but Jose should know.

"Psst! Psst!" The sound startles her and she nearly drops the tray as she peers down the dark hall for its origin.

"Here, dolly . . ." Manuel Brito whispers. "Shh! Quietly now. Come in, dolly."

Damaris sets the tray on the floor outside Manuel's door and enters the tiny room cluttered with furniture salvaged from his house: a broom and carpet sweeper, gold-painted praying hands, a blue-and-white Virgin Mary, and a huge bag of rice.

He gestures for her to take the easy chair while he sits on the bed.

"Know whose birthday's coming up?" he asks.

"Lincoln and Washington. Just 'cause I dropped out of school doesn't mean I'm stupid."

"Now, don't get all huffy. I ain't testing you. It's Jose. Be sixty-four on February fifth and I'm thinking we might have a party."

"That'd be nice."

"I'm thinking you can bake the cake, now that you're an expert at cooking."

"My cakes sink in the middle."

"Don't worry. Her favorite's got a hole in the middle. Angel food with frosting dribbled on top."

"Well . . . I'll give it a try. For dinner?"

"Her crew of kids got some shindig planned for dinner."

"How about tea, an afternoon tea?"

"Sounds a bit dowdy, but . . . what the heck . . . it'll do."

On the morning of February 5, Damaris times her cake preparations to coincide with Jose's biweekly expedition to the A&P; pleads morning sickness to excuse herself from the trip.

"This will be strictly by the book," she tells Manuel, who hovers over her as she flips to the recipe in *The Boston Cooking School Cookbook*.

"Eight egg whites! What'll we do with the yolks?"

They decide, after some discussion, to set them aside in a foil-covered bowl and let Jose determine their fate.

"You find the cream of tartar and vanilla; I'll beat the whites."

At noon, Damaris hides the cake, rather gloriously successful in spite of the time it took to beat the whites, in the dining room buffet. The pale green Limoges tea set sparkles, the coffeepot stands ready to plug in, the residents are alerted to time and to place. Only Miss Winifred declines.

"Much as I love that woman . . ." she protests, as she tugs her bed jacket tighter around her.

"I'll dress you in one of these outfits," Damaris says, fingering the soft, silk cloth of the dresses in the closet. "They look practically new."

"I think most of them were purchased during the war. And I'm talking number one." Suddenly the older woman sits up in bed, a sparkle in her eyes. "Find me a light blue dress with rhinestone buttons."

Damaris scrapes the hangers across the metal bar.

"Don't see it." Intending to lure the woman into action, she lies. The rhinestones glimmer behind a sealskin coat.

"In the back, darlin'. Keep going."

"No such dress here."

"Are you blind?" And she tumbles out of bed and ambles to the closet. "Let's see. Oh, look at this. Wore this red silk to the dance where Armand and I . . . and this green taffeta . . . that party in Onset back in thirty-seven. 'Forgotten memories rise . . .' to quote myself. 'As we yearn for times lost—laughter—green, wet earth—love hidden in the quick dark—love abandoned in the hiss of long indifference.' Well . . . here it is, right in front of you. I swear you'd lose your head if it wasn't screwed on tight."

She removes a broadly cut 1920s dress with a swatch of material gathered at the thigh to create a low waist and uneven hem.

"Try it on."

"Well, I don't know . . ." Embarrassed to disrobe in front of the old lady, to reveal her pale, stretch-marked flesh, Damaris hesitates, but Miss Winifred insists.

"Stunning," Miss Winifred says, as she tucks in the neck lining, adjusts the fall of the skirt, and Damaris admits the dress is elegant and certainly suitable for a tea.

"To the dressing table!" Miss Winifred says, pointing her finger with a flourish.

They face each other on two chairs in front of the mahogany dressing table topped by three mirrors and cluttered with tin boxes of jewelry and makeup.

Miss Winifred opens box after box of rouge and shadow, holds the colors up to Damaris's cheeks and eyes, discards this one, then that, until she finds the perfect shade.

"Sit still now."

The old fingers press against Damaris's skin to paint the creamy berry tone on her cheeks, to layer the ultramarine shadow onto her quivering eyelids.

"And for the lips, a titch of this newfangled white gloss. Give you that come-hither look."

Damaris laughs. "No one I want to come-hither except you, Miss Winifred. Come-hither to tea."

"After this escapade, you may call me Winnie."

"Now it's my turn to doll you up," Damaris says, and she sorts through the boxes of paint. Crimson for the ancient cheeks, a touch of black above the rheumy eyes, and, at Miss Winnie's request, a set of false eyelashes. "Take a look," Damaris says, and she holds up a small mirror for a side view.

"Takes ten years off me," Miss Winnie says, as she squints into the glass.

"Glamorous enough for a party."

"I wouldn't go that far."

"Not even for Jose?"

Miss Winnie peers into the mirror, runs her fingers over her barren gums. "It would mean digging out those unbearable dentures. Oh, well . . ." She sighs. "Tell you what, darlin'. We'll strike a deal."

"Deal?"

"I'll come to the party if you . . ."—she pauses, a gleam in her eye—". . . tell me who the father is."

"That's not fair."

"All's fair in love, so they say."

"I don't think so."

"We're both giving a little."

"Sounds like a lot to me."

"Let me guess, then," Miss Winnie says, and she places her hand on Damaris's knee. "Logan Perth."

Damaris drops the mirror. Luckily it doesn't break, but even if it had, things could not be worse.

"Logan?" Damaris repeats, in a whisper. She stares at Miss Winnie's gnarled fingers against her knee. They're covered with some sort of barnaclelike growths.

"A bit psychic I am. Besides, I saw you two together on the Fourth of July. Sensed what was going on."

"I don't believe in that psychic stuff."

"Logan and I talked many times."

"And he told you about me?" she asks, surprised to hear he had spoken of her, eager to know what he said.

"I'm sure he'd want to know about this."

Damaris sighs, close to tears. The dressing-table mirror reflects her own ghoulish face and that of the aged one beside her. She supposes it doesn't really matter; in fact, she feels somewhat relieved that someone besides her grandparents know, relieved but embarrassed to look Miss Winnie in the eye.

"Does this mean you'll come to the party?"

"Changing the subject, eh?"

Silence.

"Anytime you want to talk, I'm here." Miss Winnie gives the girl's knee a squeeze. "Now, then, what'll I wear?"

They choose a full-length green ball gown to hide the long johns, a pair of slippers never out of the box, a strand of pearls so opalescent Damaris is certain they are real.

At a quarter till two, both of them drenched in Miss Winnie's favorite tea-rose perfume, they slowly descend the broad front stairway and join the gathering in the parlor. All is ready: the tea steeped, the coffee percolated, the cake mounted regally on a green glass cake plate.

Pink, yellow, and orange balloons bob on their strings, tied to the overhead light fixture, to the legs of tables, to the arms of chairs.

There is a gasp as Damaris enters, escorting the older woman.

"Wonders never cease!" Connie Grouse exclaims.

Josiah Walters offers Miss Winnie his chair by the fireplace, winking all the time, though Damaris is uncertain if this is in acknowledgment of her success or merely nervousness.

"Surprise!" they shout together, as Manuel enters with Jose and they join in a somewhat shaky rendition of "Happy Birthday."

"Lord have mercy, girl, where'd you find that getup?" Jose says, holding her sides with laughter, until she sees Miss Cabot.

"Why, I'd never believed it if I hadn't seen it with my own eyes," she says. "This *is* a birthday treat!" And with that she warmly embraces the pale woman by the fireplace.

"May you enjoy as many birthdays as I have," Miss Winnie says.

Thirty minutes later, all that remains of the cake are one sagging slice and many crumbs.

"Now that Damaris can cook and clean," Miss Grouse says, "all she needs is a husband."

Damaris squirms in her chair as the others nod and murmur in agreement.

"I got a grandson about your age," Manuel says in a loud voice, as he leans toward Damaris. "How about a blind date?"

Everyone has a plan for Damaris's life. Everyone knows better than she how to live.

"Mr. Walters is a bachelor. Perhaps he'll come to the rescue," Miss Grouse says, causing Josiah to stammer and blush.

Manuel spills his coffee as he rises from his chair. "All in favor say 'aye.' "

"Leave the poor girl alone," Jose says, and she reprimands Manuel rapidly in Crioulo while she wipes the damp spot on his trousers.

"A baby without a father, oh, so sad, so sad," Manuel says.

To divert their attention, Jose displays her gifts: a knitted shawl from Miss Grouse, a natural-foods cookbook from Josiah, silver pierced earrings from Damaris.

Josiah stacks records on the turntable. "How about Perry Como?" he asks. Just as Como enters his rendition of "Blue Skies" they hear a quiet sobbing. Miss Winnie slumps in her chair, her plate slides down her shimmery dress to the floor, her thin chest trembles.

"Been a long visit for her," Josiah says. "Hasn't the stamina of the rest of us."

Jose and Josiah each take one of the crone's arms and lift her onto her feet.

"Your presence is a gift I don't take lightly," Jose says, as she accompanies her upstairs. "The best of the day, know what I mean? Best?"

Once it becomes clear Grand-pere will not relent one way or the other, Grandmother begins to make surreptitious visits.

"Any mail for me?" Damaris can't help but ask, first thing. Grandmother always shrugs, comes up empty-handed. Might the letter have been lost? Or left lying on the kitchen table by the ever more frequently forgetful Grandmother?

One Saturday Grandmother enters Damaris's room with a sack of groceries and the fragrance of peppermint Chiclets.

"I hope no one saw me," she says. "He still doesn't know I come." She sets the sack on the table, puts her arms around Damaris, hugs her firmly. The girl anticipates this hug all week; it feels so good.

"Sit, sit," the older woman says, when Damaris reaches for the groceries. Lightly touching the tip of the girl's elbow, Grandmother pushes her toward the bed. This is what Damaris thinks of when she thinks of being pregnant. Someone rushing about to make her comfortable.

Grandmother removes three grapefruits, two packages of Fig Newtons, and a box of wheat flakes from the sack and stacks them in the cupboard beside the closet.

"A grapefruit half every morning is what you need for the baby's complexion, or so my mother used to say."

"Does it work?"

"Your father was the prettiest baby in North Osprey."

"What's it like, having a baby?"

Grandmother slams the cabinet door shut and folds the grocery sack, pressing the creases firmly. "You're far too young to be in this condition, if you ask me, but you didn't."

"How did you feel when it came near the end, near time for him to be born?"

Grandmother clucks her tongue. "I don't hold with complaints and moanings." The old woman sits beside Damaris on the bed. "It's hard to tell you what to expect, you see. When it's over you can't remember."

Damaris curls up and rests her head against her grandmother's shoulder. "Tell me a story. Tell me again how I was born."

Grandmother clears her throat and sets her feet firmly on the floor, as if readying for an inquisition.

"Your mother had to do everything her way," she says with a touch of indignation. "After she married your father, all she could think of was having a baby. 'Wait until you're established,' I said time and again, but she acted as if I didn't know what was what."

Grandmother places her hand on Damaris's forehead and the girl closes her eyes as the warm fingers move across her skin.

"As soon as Twyla became pregnant, after several years of trying, I might add, she became helpless. She couldn't do this, couldn't do that. What she'd have done if we hadn't lived nearby, I don't know."

Damaris opens her eyes halfway and watches her grandmother. "Tell me the end when I'm born. That part." This is the part Damaris loves, the part about the marsh.

"As I've told you many times before, after all that helplessness, when your mother got into her last months she took to walking. She'd leave late in the afternoon and not return till dinner. Good for her, she claimed. Your father walked, too, and it's a lucky thing, because you arrived three weeks early. They were way out in some forsaken spot on the marsh when the labor pains began and they barely made it to the hospital in time."

Damaris reaches for Grandmother's hand. "Will you be there when I have this baby?"

Grandmother sighs, suddenly appears somewhat tired and dazed. "What, dear? What did you say?"

"Will you stay with me in the hospital?"

"We'll see. He'll relent in the end, I suppose."

"He's a mean, crusty old goat."

"*He* is not the only transgressor."

"I suppose he always walked the straight and narrow?"

Grandmother sighs again, stands, and smooths her skirt as she crosses the room to retrieve her purse.

"It's not for me to add fuel to the fire."

"Someday he'll be sorry. You tell him that. Someday he'll need me, and will I be there? Huh? You tell him that for me."

"I may not always agree with him, but he's a good man. He has a good heart," Grandmother says, as she closes the door quietly behind her.

Damaris has no more morning sickness, but is dreamy, lethargic. At the same time she has a need to make things, but doesn't know how to knit. She asks Miss Grouse to teach her, but it seems hopeless. She is left-handed, and although Miss Grouse is patient, Damaris's attention wanders. Confused by the reversal of directions, she skips stitches. The sweater has holes in places holes should not be.

She practices at night in her room in the chair by the window. Knit one, purl two. If the baby is female she can name her Pearl. Knit, purl, knit, purl, and before she realizes her hands are in her lap and she thinks of Logan, his chest rising and falling beneath his pale blue shirt, and when she looks down the yarn has unraveled; she must begin again.

She gives up knitting and tries sewing. An old-fashioned rag doll is what she yearns for. Jose donates half a yard of muslin and Damaris marks a pattern on paper, cuts and pins it to the cloth, leaving an inch for the hem. She hand-sews the pieces with large stitches; this at least she has done before.

There are old rags in the basement she washes and shreds for the stuffing. Leaving the top of the head open, she stuffs the feet, the legs, the torso, and the form becomes three-dimensional. Gold yarn for the hair, blue embroidery thread for simple eyes, pink for the nose and lips, a long dress created from material scraps, and there she is—somehow smaller and cruder than envisioned and the head flops over at the neck and hides the face, but . . . oh, well. The baby may not have a sweater, but he'll have a toy.

Night thoughts. Sometimes Damaris imagines she is going a little crazy as she feels the other human turning and thumping inside her womb, envisions cells multiplying, growing into the large-headed, small-legged, pale peach creature the books illustrate.

Sometimes the changes scare her; things are happening that she can't control. Sometimes she wishes the baby would stop growing, would die inside her or be born early and die. Is she cold-hearted? How can she contemplate such an event?

Sometimes she is hazy, as if she, too, floats through the night encased in an amniotic bubble, nourished by some unseen mother. There are moments when her lonely existence frightens her and she yearns for someone to sustain her. *Help me, help me,* she whispers to her parents in the dark, *be with me, please,* she beckons, and imagines in some way their spirits respond.

Damaris reveals she has not been sleeping well and Jose mixes a special eggnog guaranteed to cause dreamless repose. In bed, with the quilt tucked under her armpits, she sips the sweet liquid.

Josiah has loaned her a book on macrobiotics, "for the health of mother and child." Between the drink and the dense prose her eyes shut, her chin drops to her chest, her head leans toward her shoulder like the rag doll's. The book slips from her fingers.

Sometime later she awakens with cramped neck muscles and through blurry vision sees her mother standing beside the bed.

"Let's talk, darlin'," her mother says. She looks old, not like the few photos Damaris has seen of her with red hair flowing and freckles across her cheeks, but shriveled and white. Damaris blinks and squints in the light from the bed-side lamp.

"It's me, Winnie," her mother says, and Damaris unfolds from her cramped position and, yes, indeed, it is no apparition but the ancient poet herself.

"Cuzzy over. These old bones can't maintain the erect position for long."

Before the girl knows what's happening, Miss Winnie climbs into bed, fluffs a pillow behind her neck, and draws the quilt up to her chin.

"Don't worry, darlin'," she says. "My motives are purely platonic."

Damaris sighs, rests her hands on her ever-enlarging womb.

"Can you feel the child move?" Miss Winnie asks, and places her long, gnarled fingers over Damaris's.

"Ah, yes, I remember it well," the old woman says, looking directly into Damaris's eyes. "Does that surprise you?"

Damaris shrugs.

"Many years ago I, too, was encumbered by similar circumstances. I'd fallen madly in love. Ah, the grace and charm of the fellow. I'd stopped at a roadside stand to purchase cranberries and there he was. So handsome.

"We fell in love. 'Ah, love, we touched wrist to wrist—we vowed consonance.' But he was married and so, for many months, he came to my apartment in the early hours of the morning.

"I became pregnant. This was 1922, or was it twenty-three? Options were narrow. He paid for me to live in Florida for seven months, bear the child, put her up for adoption."

"Have you seen her since?"

"Haven't a clue to her whereabouts. I did what I was told. I have always regretted it. The love for man, it comes and goes. The yearning for a child abandoned stays forever."

"I'm not abandoning anyone."

"I'm worried about you."

"No need."

"What's your grandfather doing for you?"

Damaris shrugs and slides under the blanket. "I'm tired," she says, although now she's wide awake.

"Times like these, families should stick together. The child will need a man's touch."

"Your generation thought that way."

"And for good reason. The child will need a father. I urge you to write Logan."

The girl slides deeper beneath the covers. "I want to sleep."

"Do it for me, for an old lady who may not live much longer."

"That's old. That's the oldest ploy in the book."

"Let him be a father, if he will."

"I will not be the first to write!" Damaris says, frustration forcing the words out against her will. She had not meant to admit this to anyone.

"So that's it. Well, that's ridiculous, child."

The woman is going too far.

"Plain foolishness."

Damaris flings back the quilt, sets her feet on the floor, waddles to the opposite side of the bed.

"I'll help you to your room," she says, as she eases the old woman off the mattress.

"Child," Miss Winnie says, as they make their way down the hall, "do you need to be run over by a truck before you can see? The man has no idea of your situation. You must talk with him."

"Shh!" Damaris says. "You'll wake the others."

"I don't mean to be bossy," Miss Winnie continues, once they reach her room. "I haven't much, but one thing I do have is experience. Not that I'm wiser than anyone else, but time has taken me through many situations. I have worked my way through maze after maze and sometimes that helps me see. . . ."

"Thank you, Miss Winifred." The girl covers the woman with a blanket, turns out the light.

"Just one letter," Miss Winnie whispers.

Although in a few brief moments of doubt, the day in the shed, her first night at Jose's, Damaris thinks of writing to Logan first; she has no intention of following Miss Winnie's advice.

But Damaris agrees, has always thought, families should stick together, and so one warm April afternoon she walks through the village to the farm and under the shadow of the tulip tree watches the house for a time.

Finally she crosses to the back porch, stacks an armful of wood into the cloth carrier, swings open the door and there he is, dozing by the kitchen stove in the rocker. Ah, Grandpere. It's been awhile since she's seen him. In the past months she's had only occasional glimpses of him driving by in his blue station wagon.

She lifts the burner and checks the woodbox, adds a few

sticks, and clangs the burner into place, rousing the old man.

"So, it's you," he says, when his eyes adjust to the light.

The kitchen is in disarray. "What happened here?" Damaris asks, waving her hand over the cluttered table. An open loaf of Hollywood bread grows stale beside a jar of honey with a spoon stuck in it.

"Claire was in a hurry to get to the A and P, I guess. No telling what she'll come back with. Last time it was navy beans instead of the pork roast."

"It's not like Grandmother to be careless."

Grand-pere shrugs. "Mental decrepitude. Creeps up on you unexpected."

Damaris scrapes the nectar-laden spoon against the rim of the jar and fastens the lid. The loaf of bread she deposits in the breadbox on the counter. Then she removes her coat and seats herself at the table.

"No sense getting comfortable. We've got nothing to say."

"Grand-pere. Just look at me for a moment."

"No use looking at you, girl." He rocks back and forth vigorously.

"I don't know what to do."

"Seems like you've done enough."

"I was remembering when Grandmother packed a picnic lunch—I think it was crabmeat sandwiches, chips, pickles, and homemade pie. We drove a long way to some freshwater pond and no one else was there, just us, and we swam until dusk."

Grand-pere scowls and opens his mouth to speak, then changes his mind.

"I was remembering the Christmas when you made me a dollhouse with plastic panes in the windows and curtains sewn by Grandmother. It even had a miniature kitchen table like this one."

"Appeals to my sympathy will get you nowhere."

"Miss Winnie agrees with my keeping the baby. She once gave up a child."

"Who's that, now?"

"Miss Winifred Cabot. She's something like ninety years old."

Grand-pere looks Damaris in the eye. The chair becomes still; his hands grip the arms of the rocker.

"What do you two do? Sit around and gossip when you, for one, should be finishing high school?"

"Just think of that, Grand-pere. Having a baby and never seeing its face as long as you live."

"She send you here to me?"

"I've come to ask your forgiveness."

His face softens at these words. "I had such hopes for you."

But today Damaris is the one with hopes. "Didn't you make any mistakes when you were young?"

"Ah, then you admit to making a mistake?"

Damaris sits as straight as her lopsided form will allow. "I never said that."

"Giving up the child is not the only choice. You could bring the father into this."

Damaris remains silent. Sometimes she wonders if she resists contacting Logan just to oppose Grand-pere.

"I don't know where your stubborn streak comes from. Must be your mother."

"I am not the only transgressor." As soon as the words are out of her mouth, Damaris knows she has made a mistake. The intent was not to accuse, but to admit her own transgression, and somehow things have gotten mixed up.

Grand-pere rises from the rocker, retrieves her coat from the floor where it has fallen, holds it up with two hands, ready for her to slip in her arms.

"I'll not be blamed."

"If I am stubborn, I surely got it from you," Damaris says.

May his stubbornness cause him to petrify. May his mean bones calcify into rock.

Grand-pere flings the door open, nearly pushes Damaris out.

The baby rumbles and tumbles inside her as she returns home by way of the docks. On the far end of the slippery, seaweed-encrusted pier, where in warm weather fishing boats unload piles of bluefish and cod, she looks downward into the green-black depths of the hard, salty water. Just one slip, one slight leaning forward, and she might float on the crest of the choppy waves to the coast of Maine, float like a bottle with a message inside, to be discovered, message revealed.

Light glints off a lure caught in the wooden pilings. Wrapped around a mussel shell is a thin, barely visible fishing line. Logan. The closer the time comes for the baby to be born, the more she longs for him to know of her distress. She sighs, draws her shoulders back, and raises her face skyward for an unseen blessing.

The labor pains begin at dinner time on a Sunday in May as she sits by the window reading Benjamin Spock's book on child care. A blue-plaid suitcase borrowed from Jose leans against the chair, packed and ready. Under the window stands the gray perambulator, the cushion covered with a flannel sheet and soft blankets, a gift from the boarders. On the table are stacks of knitted suits, booties, and sweaters in various sizes, an elegant wardrobe created by Miss Grouse's needle-wise friends.

A soft wave of contraction fills her body. If this is it, the great pain she imagined, it isn't bad, isn't unbearable, a pale struggle.

When the muscles tense, clutch, and release, she dials her grandparents' number from the hall phone and asks them to come.

"He's shaking his head no," Grandmother says. Then she holds her hand over the mouthpiece and Damaris hears a muffled conversation.

"I won't tell her that, Franklin," Grandmother says with irritation in her voice. Then, in a whisper: "Put Jose on."

While Jose and Grandmother talk, Damaris lies on her bed. She clasps her hands in front of her breasts, intertwines her fingers to form a church, the two index fingers as the steeple; a game Grand-pere used to play with her. *Here is the church, here is the steeple, open the door and see all the people.* Then you're supposed to move your thumbs apart and wriggle your fingers, but Damaris keeps the doors closed, her fingers still.

Now the contractions change; the child pushes against her strong and forceful. The last thing she sees as she closes her eyes is Logan's painting. The fish seem to move, leap above and around one another, seem to break through the paper barrier to enter the room. Some rhythm she can't discern takes hold of her, she has no willful part in it, but wants a part, wants to catch up and have a part. The fish swim in the air as if the air is water. The child twists, turns, pushes in off rhythms and back beats as he begs for air, for light.

"Stay in there," she whispers. "Wait, wait, you baby."

A tap on the door and Jose walks in. "How far along are you?"

"I forgot to time the pains."

"Your grandmother will meet us at the hospital." Jose carries the suitcase and Damaris follows down the hall, runs her hand along the wall for balance, grasps the handrail as she staggers behind the older woman as if she, too, is old.

When they reach the hospital in Jose's orange Volkswagen, Grandmother has already arrived. She looks a bit disheveled, somehow awry, but Damaris is too anxious to give it further thought.

In the waiting room, Damaris sits between Grandmother

and Jose for a time. The nurse, a Mrs. Gibbs, questions the girl, says she's arrived too soon.

"This paragoric'll settle your stomach," Mrs. Gibbs says, and she hands Damaris a cup of orange juice spiked with the bitter-tasting medicine. "Come back when the contractions are more frequent," she adds, but Grandmother and Jose refuse to leave, insist the girl be given a bed.

Finally the nurse hands Damaris a gown and leads her to the shower. The shower room is drafty; a window opens onto an alleyway and gusts of air blow through. Too weak to close the window, she showers quickly. Who ever thought of taking a shower to have a baby?

Several hours later, Nurse Gibbs leads her to her room. A Boston medical school student sits with her throughout the labor, his hand on her stomach, a notebook in his lap, writing.

"I like your hand on my belly," she tells him. Odd to share this time with a blond, freckled stranger she'll never see again. A nameless man taking notes. Makes her feel important. Someone cares, writes it down.

"My father was a glassblower, you know, but he died," she says, chatty now, nervous.

The student nods and writes.

"Maybe that's what's inside me, a great big glass ball. Maybe I can smash it out with my fist."

This rouses him. He looks at her with his violet eyes, but when he sees her hands resting quietly by her sides he returns to his notes.

"This baby's father is an artist, too. Maybe he'll be famous. He doesn't know about the baby. I'd have told him if he'd written first. I was certain he'd write. For months and months I waited for the letter and still it hasn't come.

"Do you suppose that means anything? Do you suppose it means he doesn't love me?

"Being left-handed, I never was very good at figuring things out, and you being a doctor . . .

"Miss Winnie says I need to be run over by a truck. Grand-pere says, like the voice of doom, 'Pride goeth before a fall.'

"Well, the truth is stubbornness is a family trait from way back. Do you think I'm being stubborn to wait for a sign from the father?

" 'Love is the medium through which your wisdom will come.' That's what the Wampanoag woman told me, but let's face it, I'm foolish, let's face it, I'm ignorant, not wise."

The contractions become stronger, as Damaris chatters on. Nurse Gibbs turns her over and rubs her skin with methiolate. She pushes a needle into Damaris's back and tapes it in place, then turns her over again. Every hour the nurse shoots some novocain-like substance into her. Numb from the waist down, but awake, Damaris no longer feels the pains that come when her body flushes, when the child breaks the water, prepares to lash its way downward.

When the time is right, the orderly wheels her into a room: bright lights, clean tiles, yellow and green. Nurses stand round, eyes peer. Numb from the waist down, but awake. Feet in cold, metal stirrups. No mirror to see by, lights flash, voices murmur. "Push." The word echoes. "Push."

An early memory comes in the way memories do, among layers of thought present and past that school together like a mass of perch. One memory leaps forward, one breaks the surface—as the skull breaks through the opening between her legs:

Small, she was so small she couldn't see her feet, couldn't know herself as a being in the world. She rested in a warm place, in grass, green all around, on top of a soft cover. Her hand that she couldn't know as a hand moved back and forth before her eyes. She cried. A voice she couldn't know as her own vibrated, throbbed in the air. A face, Twyla's face in a halo of ruby, bent over her. Hands lifted her, a sweater opened, the breast offered, her lips closed around softness, softer in her mouth than anything she ever knew in her life, and she drew in the warm, sweet milk, rested in the crook of her mother's arm and drank until she became full.

"It's crowning. Relax now. No more pushing. Here's the head."

Numb from the waist down, but awake when the baby slides away, red and crying. She sits up to see. The nurse lifts the child into the air. "A boy," someone says. He is sad and beautiful, both of these. She cries. She weeps for the child and he cries too as he relinquishes his private space inside her to breathe, to writhe, to bellow with the rest of the world. Peter.

[6]

A great excitement ensues when Damaris returns with the infant. Somewhat in a daze, the small creature swathed in layers of bunting and blankets and tucked into the crook of her arm, she enters the main hall of the boardinghouse to find it festooned with blue streamers. They drift down from the mahogany banister, swoop from the brass chandelier to the doorframe, twist around the oak hall tree, and circle the umbrella stand.

Over the fireplace in the parlor hangs a crookedly lettered WELCOME HOME, PETER, and in front of the sign, beaming and eager, are Manuel, Josiah, and Connie.

"Oh, my, let me hold him," Miss Grouse says. Reluctantly, Damaris hands him over. Fragile as Limoges china, frail as a soap bubble, that's how she thinks of him.

"You forget how tiny they are," Connie Grouse says. "Of course, I never had one of my own, but I've plenty of nephews and nieces." She loosens the blankets, unzips the bunting, reveals the pink skull lightly covered in a pale moonlight fuzz.

"Look at these hands. And the nails. Like seed pearls."

72

Jose enters, encumbered with a suitcase and a sack of paper diapers.

"More in the wagon." She nods to Josiah, who retrieves a potted yellow chrysanthemum sent from the boarders, and a plastic baby carrier, a gift from Grandmother.

"Cootchie-coo," Manuel Brito says. Then he speaks to the child in Crioulo.

Peter cries. At the sound, Damaris's head begins to ache slightly. "I believe I'll introduce him to his bed," she says, taking the child upstairs.

Damaris shuffles from chore to chore like an arthritic old woman. What she would do without efficient Jose, she doesn't know. Life whizzes by and before she knows it Peter is one month old. The chores grow familiar. There are stacks of dirty diapers to wash in Jose's machine and hang on the line; white flags signaling her imprudence to the town. There are bottles to wash, sterilize, and fill with formula she concocts from canned milk.

In the hospital, Nurse Gibbs introduced the new mothers to the breast-feeding process.

"Those who wish to breast-feed, enter one at a time into the bathroom for instruction," the short, hefty nurse announced. Instruction? Wasn't it natural? Didn't you just do it?

Damaris hesitated, couldn't envision being enclosed in the tiny room with the stout, practical woman. Others entered one by one and the nurse completed her brief course and departed before Damaris arrived at a decision one way or the other.

One night, soon after coming home, Peter's cries awaken her. Too tired to descend to the kitchen, she attempts to feed him naturally. Bending low, she places the nipple of her small breast into his mouth. Her breasts are nearly dry, milkless; there is never any soaking of her shirts. Peter sucks for a moment, then cries, and Damaris quickly returns to the bottle, having left the magical key to natural feeding behind with Nurse Gibbs.

The child cries. Damaris removes the soiled diaper, coats the raw skin with oily cream, fastens the clean cloth, but he cries once again. She checks for a pin in his flesh, pats his back to relieve the gas, sits in the rocker and hums, "Sleep, little baby, don't you cry." No. She pushes him back and forth in the wicker carriage. No.

A soft rap at the door. Manuel shuffles in, leaning on his cane, his long, white nightshirt flapping around his ankles.

"I know what 'tis. Pins." He leans over the carriage.

"It's not . . ." Damaris begins, but the old man doesn't hear. Certain the child's under torture; he skims his thick fingers beneath the two safety pins.

"Well, I'll be. Usually pins with my grandkids."

He sits in the chair to wait and the child cries once more.

"Colic," a voice says. Miss Grouse, her hair in pink foam curlers, encased in a purple net.

"An enema's the solution," she advises. "Warm with a few drops of turpentine."

"I'll keep that in mind," Damaris says, as Miss Grouse leaves the room to order the equipment from the pharmacy.

"I've consulted my herbals and found the solution."

Josiah this time, his maroon-flannel robe belted tightly around him; a white-silk ascot at the neck. "A teaspoon of warm catnip tea," he says, holding up a mug of the brew. "Put a drop on your finger and let him suck. Guaranteed."

She supposes it can't hurt. Better than turpentine.

"What are you doing with your finger in that child's mouth?" A great commotion ensues as Jose appears with a hot-water bottle.

"What's-a-matter?" Jose asks Peter as she hands the bottle to Damaris and leans over the carriage to lift the child out. "You're all upset and no wonder." She scans the room. "What is this, a convention? Now, scat!"

No one budges.

Jose sighs.

"Heat," she says. "Simple as that. Tuck the bottle into the carriage under a blanket. You'll see."

They cluster around the carriage as Jose lays the fretful child on the warm blanket.

"But I tried . . ." Damaris says, feeling helpless and foolish. No one listens, least of all the child, who quiets now as Jose lightly massages his back. His arms and legs become limp, and his eyelids close, open quickly, then close again in slow motion over his pale blue eyes.

Grandmother, who continues her visits, provides a crib donated by one of the ladies of the Episcopal church. One morning Damaris finds the child on his side, when she's certain she set him to sleep on his back.

By the time he's three months old, a shock of golden hair replaces the moonlight fuzz. Each morning, he accompanies his mother on her round of chores, observes her with a solemn smile from his plastic throne.

"Show me that one's face up close," Miss Winnie says. Since she fractured her leg five months ago, Miss Winnie's been bedbound. "These old eyes can't see too far."

Damaris holds the child near, then sets him in his carrier on the trunk. She prepares a basin of water for a sponge bath.

"Just think," the old woman says. "That father is missing the child's best years. You're denying them both. And for what? Some foolishness about not writing first."

Damaris removes the pillows from behind Miss Winnie's head and stretches her out flat. She places towels under and around her to protect the bed and moistens the washcloth in the tepid water.

"Hush up now," Damaris says. "Can't wash your face when you're chattering." She wipes the skin, translucent as birch bark, on the woman's forehead. Bathes the cheekbones, the creases of the mouth, the hard, crusty skin on the nose.

"Don't forget to soften the old schnozzeroo with bag balm."

"Close your eyes." The eyelids quiver slightly as Damaris cleanses them with a light touch, wipes the sleepy sand from the lashes. After adding soap to the water, she removes the old woman's nightgown, covers the emaciated form with a towel.

"You aren't eating properly," Damaris says, as she traces the cloth over the woman's neck. Her collarbone protrudes from her flesh like a rebellious root from the ground. Lately the meal trays are barely touched. She subsists on a few cubes of cherry Jell-O, cups of vegetable broth.

"Lift that breast now. I sweat."

Damaris removes lint from under the breasts, lifts the arm to cleanse the armpit, dries her, and moves the towel up to bathe the lower extremities.

"I want you to notice those legs. Everyone says they look like a young girl's. Never did need to shave, smooth as an egg."

When Miss Winnie first fell and the leg was encased in plaster, she revealed how she had loved to dance at the Bournehurst Ballroom in Buzzards Bay.

Keep on dancing, Damaris had written on the cast, and when Miss Winnie had looked despondent, she added, *in your heart*.

"They are shapely, indeed. Now, let's roll you over."

A removable cast now protects the injured leg. The bones are as fragile as melting icicles. Damaris assists Miss Winnie onto her side. She curls up, fetus style, knees to chest. The old back is wrinkled and red where she lies against the lamb's-wool padding to help prevent bedsores. Her spine curves like an elephant's backbone, rises up and out of the taut skin.

"That water's cooled off now."

Damaris adds hot water to the basin. Peter whimpers.

"That's okay, Peter. I'm right here," Damaris says, and then she bathes Miss Winnie's back, creams and massages the skin.

"Best part of the day," Miss Winnie says, with a sigh of pleasure.

When they finish and Miss Winnie wears a fresh gown, Damaris assists her into a sitting position, props pillows at her side and back. Her legs dangle over the bed to rest on a footstool.

"Sit," the old woman says, as she pats the mattress beside her.

With a glance at the now napping child, Damaris reluctantly sits and awaits the lecture that usually follows; further advice as to why Damaris must stop being so childish, why she must write to Logan.

"Say the Twenty-third Psalm with me, darlin'," Miss Winnie says.

"I don't believe I know it," Damaris says, relieved there will be no lecture, but concerned about her lack of knowledge.

"There's a card with the words under the dresser scarf."

Damaris retrieves the card and Miss Winnie clasps the girl's hand tightly as they say the words together.

" 'He maketh me to lie down in green pastures,' " they intone. " 'Yea, though I walk through the valley of the shadow of death, I will fear no evil.' "

"Valley of the shadow . . ." At these words Damaris sees as if for the first time how frail Miss Winnie's body has become, understands the bones will remain fragile forever, will not mend. The skin will not regain its protective resilience. The clenched throat and shrunken belly reject food as if to say *enough, enough.*

Peter stirs, awakens, begins to whimper. Boisterous in his movement toward growth, his bellows disrupt their chant by "dwell in the house of the Lord forever."

Damaris turns to the old woman, begins to speak. Her voice, shaky and faint, reveals her new knowledge.

"Let's get . . . let's get you situated so I can tend to that one."

Damaris covers Miss Winnie lightly with a cotton sheet as, silent on her path toward decay, the faded woman eases into a reclining position.

One morning after Miss Winnie and Peter have both been fed, bathed, and set to their naps, Damaris sits at the kitchen table and stares into a mug of peppermint tea. Cold peppermint tea, as she's hovered over its menthol for twenty minutes or so.

"What's the matter with you?" Jose asks, as she enters the room with a bucket of hot water and the old-fashioned rag mop she uses on the floors. "Looks like you're about to jump right into that cup and drown your misery." She sets the bucket down, leans the mop against the wall, and sits next to the girl. "Dejected, that's the word for it. Looking mighty dejected, and no wonder. How old are you, anyway?"

Damaris shrugs. "Ninety, I think."

"And you look about ninety. What you need is time off. Let me watch Peter some mornings so you can skedaddle."

Damaris frowns.

"Don't you think I can tend a child after nine of my own?"

"It's not that."

"Then what?"

"I'll think it over," she says, hoping Jose will let the matter fall; but she won't. At dinner one night she announces that "getting this gal away from the house is like prying a reluctant mussel off its slimy old rock."

In the end, Damaris acquiesces. At first she spends twenty minutes walking through the village, thinks of Peter, hurries home to ensure his fragile chest still inflates and deflates. But after awhile, she relaxes, appreciates the time. She takes to walking farther and farther out Old County Road until one day she finds herself two miles away in the next village, in front of the spare-no-nonsense facade of the Quaker Meetinghouse.

She enters and slides into a pew, sits with the quiet, the dark wood, and plain, white walls. She admires the many-paned window at the front where in Grandmother's church the pulpit would stand.

From where she sits, only the sky appears through the clear glass. It's a little like what she imagines looking out an airplane would be like. Today the sky is full of clouds she will never forget. Rolls and rolls of matter swell like pictures of bomb clouds, with piercingly white rounds and deep shadows that draw her into their moisture. Unlike bomb clouds, these emit peace, a sense of movement and change. Quiet turbulence. That summer she returns often to the church and sits in the bare wooden pew, resting, gazing out the window.

"Mail for you," Jose says, one day early in September. She hands the girl the letter with a flick of her wrist. Her eyes glisten like a frog's about to catch his dinner.

With a puzzled expression, Damaris examines the envelope, handmade from a brown grocery bag and decorated with Logan's crazy art.

"See?" Jose says. Her inquisitive face hovers at Damaris's elbow and she points her lumpy finger, newly afflicted with arthritis, at the address. "It says 'Damaris Bishop, in care of Jose Santos's boardinghouse.' It's yours, all right."

"I can read," Damaris says, and she jams the envelope into

her pocket. Affecting a whistle, she strolls onto the back porch. Underneath, she somehow knew he would write, his longing for her too much to bear, no doubt. But she expected the letter to arrive at the farm. That was the address he knew. Glancing over her shoulder to ensure she's alone, she stares at the envelope once more, withdraws the letter, reads it with trembling hands.

September 2, 1967
Dear Damaris,
Miss Cabot wrote to me of your distress. How I wish I'd known sooner. If circumstances were different, I'd come immediately to see you and the child. Peter, she writes. But my father is quite ill and needs continual care. There is no one to take my place at the moment. And so, I beg you to come here. I have enclosed a bus ticket to Fairweather Harbor. Please write and let me know when to expect you. And I do expect you and welcome you to come. I will write upon receipt of your schedule, regarding directions for reaching Perth Isle.
                              With love and concern,
                                             Logan

Why, Logan didn't write because of longing for Damaris. He wrote from guilt, not love! He wrote because Miss Winnie asked him to! That conniving old, doddering old, interfering old witch. How could she betray Damaris this way?

She crunches the letter into her pocket, paces back and forth on the porch under the shadow of the oak, breathes deeply. Best to breathe a bit before confronting the woman.

Rereading the note, she ignites once more. Elbows thump against the wall, feet trip against the treads as she climbs the narrow back stairs, letter clutched in hand.

Temper, temper, she tells herself as she stands before the crone's door. A mild knock. Then she flings the door open so hard it thuds against the wall.

Even in summer the windows are closed. The silent room swelters with heat, the air is as compressed as in a tomb.

"Now, what do you mean?" she begins. The letter crackles like ice cubes in warm water as she waves it in the air. "How dare you . . ." she says, then stops cold.

The antiquarian, a shriveled mound in the big, double bed, makes no response. Lying on her side facing the door, her feet aim for the edge of the mattress as if she is about to rise up and head off somewhere.

"Miss Winifred," Damaris says, in a whisper. Frowning, she tiptoes to the bed, bends over the pale woman, whispers her name once more. Moments later, the letter still clutched in her fist, she shouts for Jose from the top of the stairs.

Later that day, once Miss Winifred Cabot has been transferred to the Nickerson Funeral Parlor, Damaris throws open the windows to air out the stuffy room. She can almost see the trapped heat rush through the screen into the September afternoon. Outside on a branch of the oak tree, a wren sits with a worm dangling from her beak, looks this way and that.

Damaris wanders through the room, straightens the clutter, drapes Miss Winnie's pink bed jacket over her shoulders. The soft, silky material smells faintly of tea roses and lobelia tincture. *Miss Winnie,* Damaris whispers silently as she removes the glass stopper from the tea-rose vial and douses her wrists with the sad, summery perfume.

[7]

The ferry hums through the water. On the deck, Damaris braces herself against the rail, her face damp with sea mist, Miss Winnie's sealskin coat on her back. "Colder than an Eskimo's nose up north," Jose told her before she left, and so Damaris overdresses in October for the sake of December. Peter, five months old and wrapped in a new quilted snowsuit, clutches his rag doll, his eyes apprehensive.

After Miss Winnie died, Jose found a letter for Damaris, bequeathing her a closet full of clothes and ten shoe boxes of poems. The letter implored the girl once again to visit Logan:

> If you are reading this letter it means I haven't lived long enough to tell you in person, which I'd rather do. By way of explanation, I got tired of waiting for you to be sensible. I took the situation into my own failing hands. It didn't appear anyone else was about to, and that child

needs a father. My last wish, my dying wish, is for you to give Logan a try, assuming he responds, and I do.

All my love,
Winnie

Damaris hesitated a month longer. At first she'd been upset that Logan had written only at Miss Winnie's instigation. But after a time, she realized that to live with Logan was what she imagined she wanted all along, ever since the day at Italo's Fourth of July picnic when she longed to follow Logan through the world. And she convinced herself it didn't really matter how it came about, whether by Logan's desire or Miss Winnie's manipulation; the end was the same.

Besides, she had nearly depleted her savings; income had ceased when Miss Winnie died. And so, looking for rescue, longing for love, she wrote to Logan, set a date for their arrival.

Damaris thought Grand-pere would be happy at her departure with the child. She was doing what he had asked, bringing the father into the picture. For once, she had made a decision that should please him. And at first, he had seemed pleased.

"At last she's doing something sensible," he told Grandmother, and Grandmother relayed the remark to Damaris.

But as the time came closer for her to leave, he appeared at the boardinghouse one night, asked to see the child. He whispered to the baby, took the boy in his arms, and from that moment on he changed his tune.

"You don't know what you're doing. Dragging this baby off into the unknown. Foolishness. Plain foolishness."

There was no pleasing Grand-pere, one way or the other. As soon as Damaris thought she'd gotten something nailed down, he came along with the claw end of the hammer and removed the nail.

———

Damaris carries Peter down the steps to the café below decks. On a bench by the window, protected from the mist by scratchy plastic panes, she sips hot chocolate. One minute the island ahead appears small, the next it bursts large before her vision, a dark, rough mound, stolid against the sea, like a bison bursting suddenly on the plains. A series of small islands is scattered beyond Windhaven; Logan Perth lives on one.

When they reach Windhaven, Damaris heads for the Haven Inn to find Mrs. Twine, who, Logan wrote, will provide a ride to Perth Isle.

"Jeremiah," Mrs. Twine says in a loud voice, when she comprehends who Damaris is. She has gathered her gray-streaked black hair into a loose bun on her forehead, not at the crown of her skull, where most would pin it.

"Jeremiah," she repeats, with exasperation. "Children. You'll find out soon enough." She nods at the baby and her bun quivers. "This is an easy age. They go where you take them."

A door opens on the far side of the room and a boy in his early teens emerges. No taller than Damaris, and fat, he holds a bag of crispy cheese curls in one hand and licks the yellow-coated fingers of the other.

"This lady wants to go to old man Perth's."

"Why would *anyone* want to go *there?*" he asks.

"Ours is not to reason why, ours is but to do and die," his mother says.

Jeremiah grunts and glances over his shoulder at the television.

"Come on now, baby-love. She needs to arrive before dark."

The boy sighs and disappears. The sound of the television rises, then fades, and Jeremiah returns wearing a yellow slicker.

"Ready," he says, picking up Damaris's blue-plaid suitcases borrowed from Jose.

Damaris hesitantly wends her way down the path to the dock in front of the inn. Whitecaps marble the cold, black water. A small motor boat bangs against the dock. From the porch, Mrs. Twine waves her on with a motherly gesture.

"You coming or not?" Jeremiah shouts from the boat. The motor starts, hums impatiently, and Damaris lumbers down the dock.

"What you want to see them Perths for?" the boy asks, once they are on their way. He shouts several times over the cadence of the motor before she understands. She shrugs and protects Peter's face from the salt spray with her scarf.

"They're crazy, you know. Batso," Jeremiah mouths. He belches and grins with yellow-coated teeth. Water splashes over the bow and she shivers with the wet and chill and fear of the vastness of the sea.

Twenty minutes later, Jeremiah beaches the boat, tosses the suitcases onto the sand. Damaris disembarks and questions the boy for directions.

"That's the place, lady," he says, pointing to a long tar-paper shack set back from the water atop a high bluff.

"Sure you want to stay?" He makes a guttural sound deep in his throat, then departs.

Damaris shifts Peter onto her hip, slings one of the bags over her shoulder, and walks along the beach. A worn path leads up the bluff to the shack over rough, frozen soil. On the steep climb the bag slips off her shoulder, slides partway down the path. "A glacial rock," Logan called the island, and Damaris imagines that deep in its heart ice forms, a hard knot that will never melt.

When she reaches the crest she pauses to regain her breath. Smoke pours from the chimney of the humble shack, and behind it a four-foot-high line of firewood undulates like a snake for an eighth of a mile. Scattered along the bluff are several outbuildings. Some distance away, behind a low stone wall, five or six gray tombstones lean this way and that, crooked memorials to those the island defeated.

"Logan?" Damaris asks, as she enters the shadowy cabin. A long, sooty stovepipe extends from the chimney to a bulky potbellied stove smack in the middle of the room. On top of the stove a battered kettle steams. Under the window stands an iron bedstead and in one corner on a small table a hurricane lantern waits to be lit.

"Logan?" A brown dog with three legs pushes through the blanket that curtains a doorway. A round stump protrudes from his hindquarters where the fourth leg should be. Light patches of flesh show through his thin coat. He lopes to the door and lowers his nose to the crack between door and frame.

Damaris lets the dog out, then places Peter on the bed, protecting him from the open sides with pillows.

Pictures, painted directly on the plaster, cover the walls of the room behind the blanket. Logan's art. Blues, reds, and yellows flow together into violets, oranges, greens, and muddy browns. A wide border of geometric design outlines the ceiling; birds and clouds fill the center. Her eyes return to the walls and now she depicts a forest scene: trees and animals. Like when she looks at the night sky, at first she picks out the brightest stars, the North Star or the Big Dipper; then her vision adjusts to take in the millions of others surrounding.

Another small wood stove warms a third dark room, where a man lies in bed. His skin is yellow, his eyes are glazed with cataracts, his chest rattles with his rough breathing. Old man Perth.

When she returns from the beach with her luggage, Peter is crying. She changes the child, feeds him his bottle, wonders where she will buy his milk. Against one wall is an old-fashioned ice chest kept cold, she later discovers, with ice from the pond. Where is Logan? When Peter finishes feeding, she covers them both with the sealskin coat and they sleep.

When she awakens, some creature dredged out of the sea peers down at her. Logan drips with seaweed and moisture, crackles in his mackinaw and rubber boots.

"I was afraid you wouldn't come when it got right down to it," he says. "Thought you'd write that the trip was too long."

She sits up. Somehow he is not as she remembers him; coarser, less elegant. He leans toward her, kisses her, tasting of brine, kisses her as if they are an old married couple only parted for a day, as if all the time in between didn't matter.

Logan removes his heavy yellow slicker, hangs it on a wooden hook by the door, sits on the bed. Peter, at that age when he's wary of strangers, begins to sob.

"It's your daddy, just your dad," Damaris says, in a reassuring tone. After a time the sob reduces to a whimper, then a smile, as Logan draws his finger gently across the child's skin at his throat, around his face and ears.

"I didn't know babies were like this. So soft, so small. I wish I'd known about him sooner. Why didn't you write?"

She struggles for words to explain, but they float off her tongue unformed.

"You're always so silent," he says. "Do you think I have X-ray ears? Do you think I can hear what's going on in that skull of yours?" He taps her forehead with a cold, bony finger.

Why hadn't she written? Now it does seem rather silly. Foolish, as Miss Winnie had said. How childishly she behaves sometimes without knowing why. With no energy to probe her whys, "I don't know" is the most she reveals.

"People can't understand you if you don't talk."

"I wanted you to write first." *Proof of his caring.*

He looks at her for some time with a puzzled face.

"You promised. Remember? 'I'll write,' you said, and I waited."

"I'm sorry. I never thought . . . it's just something you say, you know? 'So long. I'll write.' "

Just something you say? Then she had misunderstood. Then she is foolish. She looks down at her legs, encased in cocoons of corduroy.

"Is it always this cold in October?" she asks, to turn his attention away from herself. Logan checks the stove, adds wood to the firebox, and opens the vents to roaring.

Bacon, precious and expensive, brought the week before from the mainland, sizzles in the cast-iron skillet on top of the stove. Damaris turns the crisping pieces with a fork. She has lived with Logan for two weeks and they move through the daily chores without stress, as if they have known each other for years.

"Breakfast ready?" Logan asks, as he comes through the blanket. He rises early to tend the fire, care for his father, organize his fishing gear. In good weather he fishes with his friend Billy Flynn; even in winter they fish through the ice or set out for ice-free waters in Billy's fishing vessel, *The Dotty*.

"How's your father?" She pours eggs into the pan and stirs them with the spatula. By now the tiny three-room shack is as familiar as Jose's, almost as familiar as Grand-pere's. The discomforts inherent on the island, the kerosene lanterns, the hauling of water from the pump, are becoming routine, though the outhouse is something she imagines will take *some* getting used to.

"He calls me by his father's name," Logan answers.

Damaris arranges bacon on a plate, then turns the eggs until lightly done, moist, the way Logan likes them.

Peter sleeps on the floor in a large wooden fish crate lined with pillows. Skate, the dog, sleeps beside him. Once Logan departs, Damaris begins the chores. Diapers soak overnight in a large metal bucket. She removes one from the freezing water, twists the cloth, dips it into another bucket of clean, warm water heated on the stove. She rubs the diaper against a metal washboard, dips it again, wrings it out, and pegs it to the line that extends from one side of the room to the other. The old man shouts "heah!" from the back room before she has scrubbed a dozen.

His body lies heavy on her hands. Three, four times a day she adjusts his position. A bedsore opens into his flesh at the tailbone, cuts through the skin like a borer, digs its way to the bone. She squeezes salve onto her finger and dabs the tender, reddened spot.

"No more," he says. "Leave me alone."

"Just a bit longer," she replies, and pushes him to the far edge of the bed, withdraws the sheepskin square, and shakes it. Replacing the sheepskin under his buttocks, she rolls him partway onto the square, props his back with pillows.

"Who are you?" he shouts when she covers him with the quilts, adjusting them for the healing air to dry the sore. She whispers her name in his ear, his blind eyes close, his face relaxes into sleep.

At night when Peter and old man Perth sleep, Damaris and Logan crawl under the red-and-black-checked blanket in the sagging bed. "Are you all right?" he asks, when he lifts her flowered nightgown, moves his hand along her body. His skin is rough, scaly, chapped; his nails are rimmed with permanent black from years of working with mackerel and herring, with the recalcitrant garden soil. "Do you like to make love?"

"I'm glad I came," she says, but most often she is cold, down in her bones. They are frozen, the marrow is ice, her torso will crack like Miss Winnie's leg.

"Touch me here," she says, and moves his hand, though her body no longer pines for his as it had last summer. Somehow the body knows what the mind will not discern. After a time, she shifts her position to face the window. He moves with her, against her, presses into her from behind.

"When shall we get married?" he asks later, as he kisses her neck.

"Married?"

"You don't expect me to live in sin, do you?" Playfully he tugs a strand of her shimmery hair. "What do you think?"

"If you'd asked before . . . in September . . ." If he'd asked in September, they'd be married, bound for better or for worse. She'd loved him then, but now she's unsure. Through the window the full moon brightens the room; its celestial light probes the darkest corners. Sometimes she wonders why she is here. She never dreamed of such cold, never realized what Logan meant when he said no electricity, no plumbing, no phone. Lately she longs for home, envisions the farmhouse, silvery-gray in the moonlight, her grandparents dining in companionship at the kitchen table, solid in their love.

"I never thought," Logan says, "we had anything other than a summer romance. And now Peter . . . he changes everything."

"I'm sleepy," she says, to avoid his question for which she has no response. But when he moves away, turns his back and snores, she crawls over him out of the bed.

In the sparsely furnished painted room that serves as a sort of parlor, she lights a kerosene lantern and, in its faint glow, opens a book. This morning she trimmed wicks, washed smokey chimneys with sudsy water, filled the globes with kerosene from the huge container in a shed out back.

The book, one of a hundred or so left behind by Logan's mother, is *Anne of Green Gables*. The pages are yellow and to read in the flickering flame she holds the book at an angle and tips her head.

Before his father became ill, Logan spent the long winter evenings adding bit by bit to the walls. In the lantern light they are mysterious, almost scary, when she forgets they are there and looks up from the world of Avonlea to be confronted by the fierce eye of a hawk, amused by the striped tail of a skunk. *His art lured her to him; it's his fantasy paintings she loves.*

After a time, the smell of burning oil overwhelms her, her eyes tire quickly, her face becomes greasy, one cheek warms where it turns toward the flame. She completes a chapter, marks the page.

Fur coat over her nightgown, boots on her feet, flashlight in hand, she ensures Peter sleeps, then opens the door. Skate rumbles outside behind her.

Once on the beach, she runs across the hard, wet sand. The dog follows, but later pants, drops back. She runs to the stand of pines, then walks to the far point of the island. She climbs a large, Ice Age boulder. In the moonlight she discerns a long, slick form lying on a rock that juts into the sea. A mermaid? A seal? Of course, a seal. She calls as loud as she can, and the seal, dark eyes flashing in the moonlight, slides off the rock, bobs in the water.

On her return, she stops in the graveyard, flashes the light on the stones:

Mary Hildah Perth
1897–1956
A finer woman never lived,
what she had, she did give.

J. Wing Peabody
1800–1875
Fearless farmer and fisherman he,
he died with sorrow and lived with glee.

Mary Perth
June–July 1900
Her stay on earth was sadly brief,
we mourn her passing with solemn grief.

The other stones are old and moss covered; she cannot decipher their message.

The axe splits the wood with one blow. It crunches like crisp celery. Logan sweats in spite of the cold. Once more they work together, side by side, as Damaris loads wood into a barrow and wheels it to the cabin door. Thanks to Logan, a wool jacket replaces the ridiculous fur coat. He has money now from the sale of the Cape Cod land.

"Come spring, I'll make some changes around here," he assures her. Shingles to bar the wind; some sort of indoor toilet he read about in a gardening magazine, indoor plumbing.

When Logan has split and stacked the wood beside the door, he cleans the cod for dinner. The fish scales look like the flecks of mica Damaris finds in the rocks on the island. Mica glints when the sun shines, gives the illusion of heat and light, is warm to the touch. The only warmth in Maine, she thinks. She peels off thick chunks, sets them on the windowsill to catch the light, separates thin layers with her thumbnail, and presses the glinty mineral onto her skin.

"Much more and you'd look like a mermaid," Logan says, and gives her the idea of gluing mica onto a fish-shaped cardboard mobile to hang above Peter's crate.

Peter crawls throughout the house now, follows Skate across the floor, follows Damaris into old man Perth's room when she feeds him his fish mash. The mattress sags as Damaris places Peter on the bed. The child touches the old man's hand.

"Who's that, Mary?" the blind man says. "Is it Logan?" No matter how often she repeats their names, the confused man calls her by his wife's name, Mary; the child, Logan. Old man Perth weakens each day, and Damaris, familiar with such decline, suspects he moves toward death.

As the mercury descends, the adults bathe in the dented tin tub every three days at most, for it takes a long time to fill the basin with enough hot water for their large bodies.

But Logan takes it on himself to bathe Peter more often. He drags the tub out from behind the stove, sets the canning kettle full of water on to heat.

From somewhere he produces bath toys. One, a mottled rubber ball Damaris suspects once was Skate's, he boils in a saucepan and claims is "perfectly clean." He finds a carved wooden sailboat from his childhood, the mast long since broken, a plastic cup and spoons, and they're all set.

Stoking the fire as hot as possible, he has the towels at the ready when he calls, "Bath time," and Peter, fond of water, crawls eagerly toward the tub.

Logan removes the child's clothes, tests the water, dips him in gently. Peter squeals with glee. The boy kicks, splashes Logan, who laughs, so seldom he laughs. He soaps the small body, rinses him, and they play until the child shivers, begins to turn blue.

Winter arrives in a flurry of snowflakes; enough to layer the ground in several inches of white. The wind blows perpetually; the house on the bluff is as snug as a child's house of sticks. Every now and then, Damaris uncorks the small vial of Miss Winnie's tea-rose perfume for a whiff of spring, for the comfort of the old woman's scent.

Cooking becomes Damaris's favorite chore and she lingers by the stove, warming both the food and her hands. In free moments she sits in a chair in front of the stove and toasts her feet on the oven.

One morning in early December, Damaris awakens from the sound of Peter's cries. His hands wave in the air like small branches in a storm. She stokes the stove, removes his bottle from the icebox, heats it in a pan of water. When she lifts the child into her arms, his head, warm from crying, rests against her neck.

The bars of the rocker press into her back as she tries to feed him. Sharp nails dig into her arm and he spits the milk onto his flannel pajamas. He shudders and gasps for air, his breathing is rapid and difficult, his eyelids quiver, the skin white and veined, a faint membrane. She rocks harder, thinking to soothe him, but the motion aggravates his distress.

As the light comes in from the morning sun, she scans Logan's thin, hard face. He snores beneath the mound of checked wool. One hand rests under his cheek, the fingers extend as if he holds a platter of cod. The room is cold with the first light, as the rising sun draws the minimal warmth of the earth into itself.

Logan clears his throat, stares at her from the bed.

"It's late," she says. "Past five, I think."

"Flynn's laid up with the flu. We're not going out for a few days." He reaches for his wool shirt and jeans.

"What's wrong with the child?"

She shrugs and they talk softly for a time. Lulled by their conversation, Peter sleeps at last.

"Isn't there something you can do about the draft?" she asks, after putting the child to bed.

"Come here." He rubs her fingers against the wall. Tucked between the boards is some kind of wadding.

"Spent three winters doing that. You should have been here before."

No wonder Peter coughs; illness comes on the wind. She's been ill ever since she came. Not coughs or sores, but some kind of lethargy, some kind of cold, cold ache inside weighs her down.

After breakfast, Logan fills the woodbox and the water buckets. Most often Peter rises around seven to play with Skate, to crawl about, investigating the nooks and crannies of the cabin. This morning he sleeps without a stir until noon. He refuses his food. Damaris kisses his dry mouth, usually moist with saliva and milk. He coughs weakly and gasps for air.

"Feel his head. See what you think."

"Probably the flu, like Flynn."

They take turns holding and rocking the child throughout the day. By supper, Peter has slept fitfully in their arms, but his head still burns with the fever, his cheeks flush, blisters form on his lips.

"We've got to do something," Damaris says. "Fix a tub of water. We'll dip him, break the fever."

Hot water or cold? That is the question, and neither knows the answer. They undress the child and place him in a warm bath, a temperate compromise. He howls and squirms as she swishes water over him, rubs the creases in his legs, his belly, his arms. No pleasure this bath.

Logan dries the child vigorously with the towel. They swaddle him in flannel blankets and place him in the center of the iron bed. He sleeps restlessly in the hollow of the mattress, wakes as they are about to retire.

All night Damaris listens to the wind tear at the land, the sea beat on the shore below, as she rocks the child. At some point the night sounds increase, the surf lashes fiercely, as if the ocean is at the door.

Peter coughs every now and then; his body shivers and sweats. Exhausted, she cools his hot fingers in her mouth.

"Doesn't look good," Logan says in the morning. "Building up a storm."

The wind sounded rough in the night, but when Damaris looks outside she is afraid. The water, black as night, chops furiously at the shore. The eastern sky colors to a dirty, brassy yellow. Whitecaps reach high in the wind and the day is gloomy with low clouds.

"If it clears this afternoon, I'll take *The Sea Whip* to Flynn's and bring back *The Dotty*. Take you both to Fairweather Harbor to the doctor."

But the storm worsens, rages for two days. Passage in Logan's fifteen-foot boat is impossible. They are stranded on a bare rock, plopped in the middle of a cross sea.

"If only you had a phone," Damaris says, bewildered by the illness, the storm, the isolation. "Jose would know what to do."

"Lines would be down by now, anyway."

One hour runs into the next. They take turns sleeping and tending to Peter and old man Perth. The child sips water every now and then. He coughs up red sputum, his breathing sounds like a pot of boiling coffee. Damaris fears the fever will dry him out like a beached starfish in the August sun.

Logan recalls his mother's old medical book and they anxiously skim the pages to identify symptoms, determine a cure. For high fever and difficult breathing the book advises the afflicted be exposed to menthol vapors.

"Menthol vapors?"

"Like Vicks Vaporub, I guess."

"Search your father's medicines."

The small, greasy bottle of Vicks is empty, but in their search through the cupboards they find jars of dried leaves. Mint. Even though they may be grasping at straws, at this point they'll try anything.

Water, green with peppermint leaves, boils in the canning

kettle. Steam rises, coats the windows. The minty odor causes her nose to run, reminds her of Grandmother's Chiclets. She holds the child as near the steam as possible without burning him.

Every so often, one or the other reaches into the jar and dumps more mint into the pot. Damaris, immobile for what seems like hours, hardly notices when Logan stokes the fire, leaves to tend to his father. Her eyelids burn; their bodies are soaked in sweat.

Peter
May–December, 1967
His stay on earth
was sadly brief,
we mourn his passing
with solemn grief

In her exhaustion, white spots appear before her eyes, appear like gravestones carved with his epitaph. Moss-encrusted thoraxes, ribs like the legs of a great centipede, femurs, tibias, fibulas, skulls parade through her imagination. What will he remember of this, if he lives to remember?

The vaporizing continues until at last Peter cries and coughs, coughs so hard his face turns red and a thick fluid emits from his mouth. Phlegm on her arms, on his nightshirt, they are covered in phlegm as if they have waded through a mass of jellyfish. The coughing ceases as suddenly as it began and the child closes his eyes to sleep.

Once the storm abates, Logan rushes them to the mainland in *The Dotty.* As they enter the hospital their reflection in the emergency-room door reveals their ordeal: hair in tangles, clothes wrinkled and twisted into odd contortions, scruffy as hermits, weary refugees shipwrecked in the storm.

"Pneumonia," Dr. McCully says.

In a private room with an oxygen tent, Peter, nearing dehydration, is fed intravenously. Damaris watches beside him in a puce-colored plastic armchair. The world is full of clamorous noise, a great confusion of sounds, a babble of voices. Nurses chatter, metal carts clank, babies cry.

Damaris's head nods, leans toward her chest; her eyes close. At the sound of Logan's voice suggesting she rest on the cot beside the crib, she snaps to attention. With little sleep for days, what will a few more hours matter?

"Got here in the nick of time," Dr. McCully says, but Damaris knows in her heart of hearts that she and Logan saved the child, that the worst occurred in the cabin. Death grinned, but was held at bay.

Once Peter is beyond danger, Logan returns to the island to relieve Flynn, who tends to his father. Damaris sleeps on the cot for five- or six-hour intervals, half aware of the nurses who whisk in and whisk out. Every now and again she rises on her elbow to peer at the child. He breathes easier now, his chest moves up and down with a smooth beat, like a cat's chest as it stretches into lanquid sleep.

Under the bright cafeteria lights she eats starchy food reminiscent of high school; she takes brief walks on the snow-covered hospital grounds, admires the Christmas tree in the hospital lobby. Christmas. She'd nearly forgotten.

Sponge-bathing as best she can in the ladies' room, she blesses its easy warmth and changes into fresh clothes brought from the island.

The island: the ice-crusted buckets of dirty diapers, the wind hissing through the cabin walls, the icehouse Logan calls the outhouse. The months on Perth Isle were like some grim book she'd read, like some throwback to archaic times, nearly pagan. She tries to envision them living there again, but imagination fails her. How can she return the child to such cold?

After several days, she telephones Jose collect.

"What's wrong?" Jose says, at the sound of Damaris's voice.

Unable to admit her mistake in coming to Maine, unable to describe the feeling that to return to Perth Isle would be a sort of death, death of her heart, Damaris asks, "Is my room still vacant?"

"It's got your name on it."

"I'm thinking of coming home." Thinking; as if she still debates the matter—never will she return to that dreary tar-paper shack.

"You need money?"

There is a pause. "I . . . I . . . uh . . ."

"No need to hem and haw. 'Yes' or 'no' will do."

"Yes."

And so it's settled. Jose will mail a money order, will pick Damaris and Peter up at the bus station once the schedule's set.

By the time Logan returns three days later in a frayed flannel shirt and patched wool trousers, Peter no longer needs oxygen, is taking nourishment by mouth.

Nothing has ever sounded as melodious as the meal cart rattling down the corridor, smelling of steam and milk. Eager as a baby bird for the worm, Peter slurps up the puréed golden squash, the deep purple plums, the buff-colored chicken that Damaris spoons into his mouth.

Logan brings in tuna sandwiches and cartons of juice from the cafeteria. The bread is stale, the crusts tough as rind, but Damaris eats now, too, as if she's been starved.

Certain she has made the right decision to leave, she is uncertain how to let Logan know. If only he could read her message on her palm, in the arch of her eyebrow, on the curl of her hesitant tongue.

"So much nicer when food is all prepared," she says, indicating the sandwich. Perhaps a few side-issue complaints will loosen her tongue, set the words flowing. "So handy to be near the grocery store. On the island, it's almost a crisis if you forget to buy an ingredient."

"Improvisation is a lesson the island teaches."

Damaris licks the tuna salad off her fingers and sips her juice. "He almost died because of your island," she says, in a matter-of-fact way, for she convinces herself this is true and that it is Logan's fault. And though part of her says he did all he could, another part of her cannot forgive him for what he could not do.

"An island doesn't cause someone to die." Logan collects the waxed paper and tosses it into the wastebasket.

"It's no place to bring up a baby," she says, still unable to voice outright her intent to leave.

Logan laughs deep in his throat, a guttural chuckle that nears a lament. "I was once a baby, born and raised on that island and alive to bear witness," he says, leaning toward her over the arm of his chair. He takes her hand, presses it between his. "You haven't been happy there," he says. "I notice, don't think I don't."

On the bedside table the thermometer sits in an aqua tube of alcohol near the box of Kleenex, the baby bottle of water, the damp washcloth. If she looks into Logan's eyes his concern might draw her into his dismal world once more, like a tornado draws houses to its center toward destruction.

"I won't return this baby to that cold shack." She glances briefly at Logan out of the corner of her eye. His body stiffens.

"Things will be better come spring."

"I'm returning to North Osprey," she says at last. She looks at him full now.

Logan is silent for a long time. By his face, faded and in need of a shave, by the way he twists his mouth, by his frown, she knows he is hurt.

He releases her hand and gazes down at the waxed green tiles of the floor. For a brief moment, Damaris remembers him as he was in the blowing room, that luminous, flame-bound amphitheater, working with Italo as her father must have done, by some mystical alchemy turning sand into glass.

Glamorous and alluring, Logan had seemed then, with the drawing power of an actor in a play. Now, backstage in the harsh glare of the dressing-room lights, he stands unadorned, makeup and costume abandoned.

Improvisation, a lesson the island teaches, Logan said. A lesson well learned after living on the rock for only three months. As iron filings gather to a magnet, her thoughts gather now into one firm message: *Leave, leave, for Peter's sake, leave.* She will improvise some sort of housing, some sort of job. What else can she do? What else can she do.

PART · II

[8]

Winter 1967–1968

"You can always change your mind and stay," Logan says a week later as they wait for the bus to depart. Encased once more in his quilted snowsuit, Peter wriggles in Logan's arms.

"You heard Dr. McCully. Peter needs a warm house, easy access to a doctor in case of complications."

Logan holds out his finger for the child to grasp, then pretends to draw it away. Peter laughs, tightens his grip.

"I'll miss this one," Logan says. He stares at Damaris, looks for a long time right into her and she knows he is trying with his look to melt the hard, cold knot of determination in her bones, which only makes her more determined.

"Come back to the island with me," he says. He removes his finger from the child's grip, runs his hand along Damaris's cheek, and she knows with his touch he is trying to pry open her hard, closed self. But it is too late. Looking for escape, she brushed with death. Looking for rescue, she found misery. There is no way to hide her foolishness. What woman in her right mind would leave the companionship of a gentle man to return to a house full of elders? It doesn't make sense, but something draws her to Osprey, some unfinished business.

"A mother knows what's best for her child," she says, reaching for Peter. The Boston bus is ready to board.

Logan removes a bank envelope from his pocket. "I want to contribute to his care."

"You don't owe us anything."

"I'll mail a check each month." He tucks the envelope into the new diaper bag purchased for the trip, kisses the child, watches as they board.

Peter's health, Damaris thinks. That's what matters.

She sits in a row with two empty seats, one for herself, one for Peter. She holds him in front of the dusty window, moves his hand up and down in a waving motion.

The bus is dirty, the fumes clog her breathing. The closer they come to the city, the more crowded the bus becomes; folks traveling for the holidays. In Portland, a large woman carrying a worn oilcloth shopping bag approaches.

"Howdy, I'm Holly," she says, and indicates her desire to sit. "Ah, that's a sweet one," Holly says, as Damaris lifts the child onto her lap. "How many you got? I got seven. In fact, excuse me here while I lean over you to wave out the window at Donald. There he is with the kids."

A small man in a red-wool jacket holds two young children in his arms. A bevy of others, varying in size like the pipes of an organ, cling to his pockets and the hem of his jacket.

"Leaving 'em all behind," Holly says. "Visiting my mother in Somerville. Give Donald a taste of mothering and me a taste of a holiday. First in years. Have a cashew?"

She opens a can of nuts, jiggles them up and down. "Where's yours at?"

Absentmindedly, Damaris takes a few cashews; uncertain what Holly means, she doesn't respond.

"Your husband, I'm talking about. Left him behind for the holidays?"

"I haven't got one of those."

"Just like my sister Sal what lives in Vermont. Five little ones. No husband. Never had one, swears she never will. Now, me, I like a steady man in my life. I like knowing I got Donald to cuddle with on a cold night, though there are some muggy nights I do wish he was elsewhere. Want to see some pictures?"

Damaris, busy dredging up a bottle of orange juice for Peter out of the diaper bag, doesn't answer, which she discovers doesn't matter one way or the other with Holly.

Holly opens an enormous leatherette purse and removes a bulging pink-and-orange cosmetics case, a can opener—"always bring my own"—a traveler's-size package of Kleenex, a thick envelope stuffed with photos.

"Now, here we have Donald and Lewis, the youngest . . ."

It could have been worse. Damaris might have been stuck with someone who'd had too much to drink and snored as she had on the trip out. Peter weighs a ton in her lap.

"And this is my Gerald. Nearly fifteen now . . ."

Fifteen. Only a few years younger than Damaris, and footloose and fancy-free by the looks of it. Damaris shifts the baby from one leg to the other, adjusts her position as much as possible in the small space.

"Here, what am I thinking, going on like this? Let me take a turn holding him."

And before Damaris can rouse herself to protest, Holly dumps everything back in her bag, stows it beneath her feet, and takes the child from his mother.

"Heezza precious one, isn't he? Well, goo."

In Boston, white and gold bulbs illuminate the store windows. Streetlights near The Common are wound round with greens. As they approach the station, Damaris slips the diaper bag over one shoulder, her bulging weekend bag over the other, and takes Peter from Holly.

"Thanks for your help. I hope you have a good Christmas with your mother."

"We never did get on together, but I figure she might not be here much longer, so . . . well, never mind my troubles. You have a good Christmas, too. It's special, you know, their first."

Exhaustion, dust, the smell of diesel fuel bring tears to Damaris's eyes. What kind of Christmas can she give the child with no money, no job, barely a place to live?

As she lumbers down the aisle, she feels like one of those journalist photographers she sees on television; huge leather bags crammed with equipment bulging out from either side. The driver assists her down the steps. Amid fumes of arriving and departing buses, Damaris waits. Inside the Cape Cod bus, the driver eats a sandwich, glances at her waiting outside, shrugs, unwilling to interrupt his meal to let her board early.

In his own good time, he crumples his lunch bag, takes a slow walk down and up the aisle, bends over now and again to collect trash from the floor.

Peter weighs two tons. The straps of the bags cut into her shoulders, binding her, pressing her earthward, holding her feet to the ground. *Keep 'em barefoot and pregnant;* Miss Winnie's voice shifting to forward position in her memory.

At last the door hisses open. With a flick of her fingers, Damaris offers the ticket from beneath the bundles she carries. Then aboard. The last of the journey.

Nothing looks as marvelous as Jose's orange Volkswagen bug idling with a rumble and a spit of exhaust at the bus station in Buzzards Bay. Leave it to Jose to be on time.

"I'd take those bags from you, but my arthritis is acting up. Can't lift a thing," Jose says, as Damaris heaves her bags into the trunk. "You got the look on your face of the mole the cat dragged in."

"Did you ever take a long journey with a baby?"

"Now, what kind of a question is that? With nine, a trip to the grocery store was a long, long journey."

Damaris rests her head against the back of the seat. She hadn't realized how much she missed Jose until now. How much she missed North Osprey. Actually, Peter slept most of the journey. Caused no problems.

"It's not your way to reveal," Jose says, "and it's not my way to pry, but if you want to talk, I'm all ears."

But what is there to say? Is there a ten-letter word for her sorrow? How can she condense her disappointments into a few sparse sentences? How can she weave the last few months with Logan into a story to tell?

Jose has prepared Damaris's old room for her; Miss Winnie's for Peter.

"Time he has a room of his own. Stuffed Winnie's paraphernalia into the closet. Horacio, my eldest, helped me take down the bed, so there's plenty of room for the crib. Now, what are your plans?"

Plans? Damaris can barely keep her eyes open, much less discuss plans. At this moment she plans nothing more than to crawl between Jose's cool white sheets smelling of salt air from hanging on the line.

"I'm home." The next morning, Damaris telephones Grandmother, who doesn't seem at all surprised by her return.

"Your grandfather's Christmas-shopping. Why don't you come over?"

Damaris wends her way through the streets, Peter strapped to her back in a baby sling, an early gift from Jose. Christmas is only three days away. Small as North Osprey is, decorations are no more elaborate than the schoolchildren's paper Christmas bulbs hanging on the post office walls. At Queen's Department Store a fringe of blue tinsel outlines the window. Inside, a zoo of large, stuffed animals models red and green baby clothes, clothes Damaris desires to buy, to wrap in blue tissue and tie with a snowflake ribbon.

Grandmother's housekeeping skills have gone downhill. Stacks of dirty dishes line the kitchen counter and clutter the floor.

In her red Christmas apron patterned with green wreaths, Grandmother hovers over a sink full of soapsuds. Her hands move back and forth in the air in the motions of washing, but she holds nothing but a dry sponge. No plate, no silver. She appears startled when Damaris opens the door.

"When did you get back?"

Damaris hugs the old woman. Frowns. "I called you a while ago. You said to come on over."

"I've been cleaning all morning," Grandmother says, changing the subject.

Cleaning?

"I'm glad you're here, dear. Let me see that one. Oh, what a sweet."

They remove Peter from his carrier, set him down to crawl.

"They grow so fast at this age. Before you know it, he'll be driving a car."

Upset by the disorder of the kitchen, Damaris examines the rest of the house. The rooms appear in reasonable order. As every year, a Christmas tree, trimmed with handmade felt ornaments sewn with sequins and lace, fills a far corner of the living room.

Reassured by the sight of the tree, Damaris returns to the kitchen to find Peter about to explore the bottles of ammonia and bleach stored in the cabinet below the sink. She lifts him up and away, holds him in one arm while she searches for an elastic band in the junk drawer to bind the cabinet doors. Once done, she realizes Grandmother has disappeared.

"Grandmother?" she hollers down the dark basement stairs.

When she opens the door of the small, unheated pantry, the cold air makes her shiver. Empty. And then through the window, a flash of red and green. Coatless and wearing her black, flowered slippers with holes in the toes, Grandmother heads for the woodpile with an axe.

Not wanting to leave the child alone, Damaris carries him outside.

"What are you doing?"

"What's it look like?" the old woman says with a scornful expression, as she attempts to split a log. "Who else will fill the woodbox while he's out chasing every skirt this side of the canal?"

"I'll take this," Damaris says, reaching for the axe, puzzled and dismayed. Grandmother has never spoken this way before. As Damaris places the axe in the shed, she resolves to speak with Grand-pere today, whether he wants to or not.

When they return to the house, Damaris washes the dishes, while Grandmother sips a cup of tea. By the time the gravel crunches under the tires of the blue station wagon, Grandmother is her old self again.

Pere emerges from the car, loaded with shopping bags. The old man emanates cold; cold waves rise from his navy blue parka like heat waves from a tar road in the summer. Once inside, he sets his bags down and scoops Peter into the air.

"Look at him. Look at this fella. Got to get some meat on these bones. He's too thin."

"He's been sick, lost some weight."

"Sick? But he's . . . ?"

"Fine now. Say hello, Grand-pere."

Peter laughs and says, "Gaa."

"Why are you here?" Grand-pere asks, once he has settled in, as if he only then remembers she should be in Maine. His voice sounds weary; there is none of his past belligerence behind the question and Damaris responds with a shrug and a brief explanation.

Later, when Grand-pere retreats to his basement work-
room, Damaris follows with Peter, afraid to leave the child
in Grandmother's care. The basement holds a musty smell,
the smell of damp cement, moist pipes. The smell of sawdust,
wood varnish, and oil.

"We need to talk about Grandmother."

Pere glowers. Reaching above his head, he snaps the
chain on the fluorescent light. On his workbench is a
wooden duck on wheels, wings and tail feathers carved with
a wavy line.

"For Peter?"

"Well, it's not for your grandmother."

"What's happening here?" she asks, touching his arm.
"Something's wrong."

Grand-pere tenses for a moment, as if debating with himself. Then he shrugs. "Claire's been . . . forgetful."

"Forgetful? I found her outside with an axe."

"Mental decrepitude," he says, as he sorts intently through
his wood-carving tools. "Misplaces what she's up to, like I've
misplaced my burnisher."

"Don't you think we should call Doc Wylie? Set up an
appointment."

"Ahead of you. As usual. First week in January."

"And about time, I'd say."

"Well, what do I know? I'm just an old man." He sighs,
removes a handkerchief from his pocket, wipes the cartilage
of his nose. "You young folks . . ." he says; his voice breaks
and he turns to look at her. "You young folks don't understand what it's like to be old." He places his hand on her
shoulder and with this gesture waives his stance as guardian
of the threshold.

Christmas Eve at Jose's. A great excitement.

"First time in years we've had a young one about," Jose
says. "Not counting my own grandkids, of course."

Originally, the elders agreed not to erect a tree that year; Miss Grouse had flown to Ohio to visit relatives and everyone else would be gone Christmas Day.

Everything changes on Peter's return. Christmas Eve morning, Jose sends Damaris and Josiah to Buzzards Bay to sort through the leftover trees for sale. Most are either tall and thin or short with sparse branches, but after some searching they find a suitable tree.

The rest of the day they spend clipping the lower branches for a wreath, setting the tree straight in the stand, no easy task, debating which side should face the room, keeping the fragile bulbs out of Peter's reach. Packages miraculously appear for Peter, and even a few for Damaris.

After dinner, everyone gathers in the parlor. Jose produces a camera and the flashbulbs hiss and crackle as she takes this shot and that. Josiah produces a bottle of brandy and even Damaris has a taste of the liquor.

"We'd be just a bunch of half-deaf old geezers," Manuel says, "if it wasn't for these angels of light." He gestures toward Damaris, seated in the easy chair, Peter at her feet.

"But for the inconstancy of woman," Josiah adds. "A toast to Damaris and the fickle heart of a lady."

What's a six-letter word for "capricious"? *Fickle.* The remark gives Damaris pause. She simply left for Peter's sake. For his safety and health. There had been no capriciousness involved, nothing as flighty as that. She had, she now admits, made a mistake in carting the child off to strange surroundings in the first place. No wonder he fell ill; his way of telling her life on the island was unsuitable. To Damaris, the admission of her mistake seems quite profound. A step toward growing up; nothing as chancy as fickle.

"I've heard tales about you and women's hearts," Jose says to Josiah.

"And all of them false," Josiah says, primly pouring himself a few more drops of brandy.

Peter, bathed and dressed in his footed pajamas, crawls swiftly toward the silvery tree.

"Whoa, now," Manuel says, and the old man rattles a present to distract the child. "Let's see what's inside."

Manuel unties the ribbon. Peter shreds the paper with a smile and a drool.

Undershirts.

Every boy's dream.

Christmas Day. Josiah departs for Boston to visit friends. Manuel and Jose traipse off to the family gathering at her daughter Agnes's, and although Jose invites Damaris several times, Damaris declines.

"Don't want you to turn into a hermit like Winnie."

At the mention of their old friend, their eyes meet in mutual sadness. Last Christmas had been Damaris's first at the boardinghouse, Miss Winnie's last.

As soon as the house is empty and quiet, Damaris drags out aluminum pots and pans for Peter to play with on the spotless kitchen floor.

On the back porch, she sorts through the discarded *North Osprey Times* for the recent issues. Then, with a cup of tea and a pair of scissors, she searches for a likely job.

In May the restaurants will advertise for waitresses, the motels for maids; but this is December. Those who work in the summer often depend on welfare in the winter; wait out the slack season at home or spend hours in the local bars.

"No high-school diploma," Damaris says to Peter, after a time. "No typing, no shorthand. What'll I do?"

The child looks up, drops the lid he's banging, crawls to Damaris's feet. He clings to her legs and she lifts him to a standing position.

"Help me with this puzzle," she says. Placing him on her lap, she wipes the drooling mouth, checks the two white flecks of teeth cutting into his gum. As he teethes on her finger she asks, "So what's a five-letter word for 'decimal unit'?"

"Gaa."

At noon, the telephone rings. Grand-pere.

"Don't get overjoyed," he says. "It's the kid I want to see."

"We come together or not at all."

"How's two o'clock, if you have no other pressing engagements?"

"You're getting weak in your old age. Weak and sentimental."

"Always the smart remark. You coming or not?"

"Two o'clock."

A frail figure wearing the Christmas apron bends over the oven. Expecting Grandmother, it takes Damaris a second or two to realize this is Grand-pere. When had he shrunk? Even three days ago he'd seemed larger, and surely it was only months ago he had towered over her, a wrathful totem.

"You're the chief cook?" she asks.

"Don't say anything, not a word," he says, as he removes the roast and carries it to the counter.

The round oak table in the rarely used dining room is set for four. On one side of the table stands an old wooden high chair with a caned seat that once held Mitchell, then Damaris. On the other side sits Grandmother with glazed, daydreamy eyes. She clangs her fork against her glass.

"Service. I want serv——" As if someone snaps his fingers, Grandmother's expression changes when Damaris enters.

"Glad you've returned from that dreadful place. Last time I saw this child, he was a newborn."

"We were here a few days ago. Don't you remember?"

Grandmother appears disheveled; her hair is matted and unbrushed; the collar of her blouse turns in, not out.

"Oh, yes," she says, tapping her forehead, as if recalling. "Of course."

"Get that one's snowsuit off," Grand-pere says, as he enters with the roast on a white, ironstone platter, "and give me a hand with the vegetables."

Damaris chops vegetables and mashes potatoes in a plastic bowl for Peter, who displays his newly acquired talent for drinking from a cup. Grandmother displays her newly acquired talent for eating in a manner reminiscent of the boys in the high-school cafeteria. She devours potatoes and green beans as if she hasn't eaten for days.

"A week ago she wandered to the center of the village and—"

"Who do you mean by 'she'?" Grandmother asks, snapping to attention.

"Yourself. Claire Elaine Bishop."

"I never did. I sat under the lamp mending your socks. It's you that wanders."

"You remember Anathea Byers, don't you? Owns Queen's?" Pere asks Damaris.

"I've been gone only three months, for goodness sake."

"Anathea appears at the door with this one—coatless. I'd been in a panic, of course."

"Don't believe a word, dear. He's covering up for his own exploits."

"It's not the first time this has happened."

"Why didn't you tell me the other day?"

"I've done some thinking since then . . . if you're old enough to be a mother, you're old enough to share—"

"Speaking of mothers," Grandmother interrupts, laughing and pointing at Peter. "If he doesn't take after his. Makes a mess out of everything."

"Mah," Peter says. Beans and gravy adorn his hair, potato drips down his cheeks. Inverted over his head, his bowl becomes a white plastic derby to accompany his smile, his voice, as it lifts into a crescendo of glee.

"Want me to move in and help?" Damaris asks a few hours later, as she heads out the door.

"That far I'll not go yet," Grand-pere says.

He never says why he relents and invites Damaris home. She guesses it's in part a longing for Peter, in part his way of telling her about Grandmother, but she never knows for sure, just knows that from Christmas Day on, she gradually becomes a part of their lives once more.

"Let me know what Doc Wylie says."

"Could be any number of things," Doc Wylie reports to Damaris on the telephone in January after Grandmother's visit. "We'll set up a series of tests. See what we can find."

"Senile dementia," Doc Wylie finally concludes.

"Mental decrepitude, like I said all along," Grand-pere mutters. "Didn't need a doctor to tell me that."

It is mid-February. Grand-pere and Damaris sit in the doctor's office in the back of his house amid dusty wooden file cabinets, stacks of books. The tests have eliminated depression, chemical imbalance, brain tumor, lung disease. . . .

"Nursing home," Doc Wylie recommends.

"Absolutely not," Grand-pere says.

"Needs twenty-four-hour care. No job for an eighty-six-year-old man, Franklin Bishop."

This is a job for Superman, Damaris thinks when she hears the doctor's pronouncement, trying to lighten its grimness with a bit of humor. *Or Superwoman, as is the case.*

"Come to it sooner or later. Sooner'll save a lot of wear and tear on you, Franklin."

"Make do somehow."

As usual, when Grand-pere makes up his mind, he does not relent with ease.

"Stubborn old cuss," Damaris says under her breath, but in her heart she agrees. Making do is better than a nursing home any day.

9

Although Damaris offers to move in once again, Pere continues to deny the need for help, and so by late February, Damaris takes a job. Word of mouth brings it her way. Town gossip—Jose's injured vocal cords the source—sends out the word that Damaris has a way with old folks.

By March, the routine is set. First thing in the morning she drops Peter off with Jose's daughter Agnes, who cares for him nearly for free; then she heads for Tabitha Tobey's.

Blind and skinny, the part-Indian "lady," as she calls herself, lives in a tiny cottage by the cranberry bog. Damaris sponge-bathes her and weaves her dry hair, black as a raven's wing, into thin braids. She cleans the cottage and drives (she is forced to take hasty driving lessons from Horacio to obtain her license) Tabitha Tobey's 1953 Rambler to the A&P.

Tabitha tells Damaris about Cyrus Wing, down the road a piece, who has gout so bad he can't walk without a cane in each hand. Cyrus Wing tells Damaris about Bertha North, who walks but is breathless by the time she makes it from the bed to the couch. There is no lack of work among these old folks, invisible to the world, tucked away in their sheltered pockets of need.

The day Damaris enters Tabitha Tobey's run-down cottage, she falls in love with the woman. Less at first with Tabitha herself, more with Tabitha's back room, crammed with old furniture (antiques to Tabitha), musty, yellowed papers (valuable historical documents), cartons of shells, baskets of rocks and . . . beach glass.

There are giant brandy snifters of green beach glass, plastic wastebaskets of white, trays of brown and blue, wine-bottle lamps filled with rainbows of shards, beach glass embedded in plastic coasters, beach glass glued to lampshades—"my version of the Tiffany."

"Where did you find so much beach glass?" Damaris asks in wonder.

When Tabitha Tobey smiles her secret smile over her toothless gums, the cheeks in her bony skull stand out like smooth new potatoes.

"No more than a fisherman reveals his favorite spot do I reveal mine."

What Tabitha does reveal is how to work with the shards.

"Blind as I am, I still have the use of my fingers, thank the good Lord," she says, and Damaris plays apprentice to Tabitha's meticulous demonstrations. "Now we dab glue on the back of the glass. Quite a bit because of the uneven shape, but never mind, it dries clear." With shaking fingers she applies the shards to a plastic Kleenex box cover.

Tabitha's humble projects add fuel to the fire that had almost died out in Damaris. That mysterious, surprising thirst for beach glass. As soon as the winter cold lifts, she tucks Peter, nearly one now, into his safety seat in Jose's orange Volkswagen and drives first to one beach, then to another and another.

As the months pass, she scours the beaches near and far at every opportunity, a sack looped through her belt to collect the sand-worn chips of glass. Her eyes become sharp; she learns to spot the shards from the distance, uncovers their presence beneath the brown-green seaweed, discovers them glinting between rocks, glinting like the rhinestones on Miss Winnie's ball gown.

By the time Peter is nineteen months old, things have gotten out of hand at the farm. Throughout the year, Damaris visits as often as possible, helps out when needed. Grandmother's decline is gradual, her wandering infrequent, her problems manageable until the end of the year, when one day Grandpere telephones, requests that Damaris come. A new problem has arisen.

When she first enters the house Damaris notices a stale odor, an odor that fades once she's been inside for a time. At the kitchen table, Pere warms his hands against a mug of tea. He shakes his head in despair.

"She's in her bedroom."

For the past ten years Grand-pere and Grandmother have slept in separate rooms. Damaris finds Grandmother seated on the edge of the mattress among soaking bed linens. A commode, new and shiny, stands beside the bed.

Damaris sits by the old woman, takes her hand gently.

"Let's get you out of your wet gown. We'll take a bath. Dress you in something clean and dry."

"We've already had a bath," the old woman says gruffly.

"Baths bear repeating," Damaris says, as she lifts the gown over Grandmother's head.

"We're clean as a whistle."

"You sit on the commode, while I fill the tub."

"Commode?" Grandmother looks about, anxious, almost fearful. "Commode?"

"Right here," Damaris says, guiding the old woman.

"Funny kind of chair. Never seen anything like this. Ethan Allen?"

As Damaris is about to leave the room, Grandmother detains her with a firm grasp, draws her near. The thin lips tremble and for a moment there is a look of knowing, a brief flicker of light in the old eyes. "My mother was like this . . ." she whispers. *Rescue me,* the eyes seem to say. *Lift me up and out of this mire.*

Damaris longs to comfort her, but before words form, the brief light fades and Grandmother is distant once more.

After the bath, Damaris seats Grandmother on the living room couch. " 'Froggie went a courtin' and he did ride, mm-mm,' " Grandmother sings to herself.

Damaris slowly enters the kitchen. For a time, she sits across from Grand-pere in silence, runs her finger round and round a tea stain on the tablecloth. The faint sound of Grandmother's song rises and fades in the distance. " 'Mm-mm, mm-mm.' "

Damaris sighs, straightens, determines to fight for this, determines not to accept any resistance.

"Time I move in."

Grand-pere agrees faster than she ever imagined he would, but then any fool can see he is near collapse.

"It's either that or the nursing home. Thought the commode would help, but this . . . this . . ."

"Incontinence?"

"Yep . . . more than I can handle."

Grand-pere stares at Damaris then and she returns the stare. When she looks into his eyes it's as if she descends into a hidden corner of his heart; she is a part of him. And when he looks back she draws him in; he is a part of her. With this look he releases the last remnant of his refusal to acknowledge her. With this look they move closer together in the skittish dance they have done for years.

"Call the police, we're being invaded. Burglars, thieves, robbers," Grandmother says the next Saturday afternoon when

Damaris pushes open the back door, two sacks of clothes in her arms.

"Now, Claire, it's Damaris. Damaris moving in," Grand-pere says. He attempts to move the old woman out of the way.

"Arrest her," Grandmother says, as Grand-pere escorts her to his rocking chair by the stove.

"Your granddaughter," he repeats, his voice weary.

Damaris sets down her sacks to help guide the resistant woman onto the seat. Grandmother kicks Damaris in the shins.

Jose's son Horacio Santos, though short, is hefty from workouts with weights. "An impressive figure of a man, if I do say so myself," as his mother describes him. Today, he helps Damaris move. At that moment he enters the kitchen, assesses the situation. He works in a nursing home, has seen this before. Quietly he sets down the boxes he carries. Patiently he introduces himself, his voice deep and soothing.

"Horacio, madam. May I assist you? Here is your chair. Face me. Now, bend your knees and ease on down."

Surprisingly, Grandmother sits, gazes into Horacio's brown eyes with a soft, coy look.

"Tea," she says. "And a spot of lemon." And as Pere hastens to fill the kettle, she sings once again:

" 'Next came in was a bumblebee, mm-mm,
Danced a jig with a two-legged flea, mm-mm.' "

"That woman needs outta here," Horacio advises Damaris, once they are beyond earshot. But Damaris knows her moving in is a silent pact of stubbornness between Pere and herself, a pact to avoid the nursing home as long as possible.

Steadily throughout the afternoon Damaris and Horacio load and unload the blue station wagon. In her two years away from the farm, Damaris accumulates three trips' worth of possessions.

By five the move is complete. "I'd ask you for dinner, but . . ." Damaris says to Horacio, nodding in Grandmother's direction.

"Got to be at work anyway. Night shift this month."

"I'll take you out for pizza soon."

"Hey. Never you mind. Someday you'll return the favor."

After the disruption of moving day, things settle into a routine. Damaris reduces, then quits entirely, her jobs in the community.

At home, chairs and cushions must be covered with plastic, as Grandmother is inevitably wet nowadays. The commode is moved from room to room in her wake, though not to much avail. It's almost as if Damaris has two youngsters to care for. Put Peter on the potty, put Grandmother on the commode. Change Peter's diapers, change Grandmother's diapers. Give Peter a bath, give Grandmother a bath. Feed Peter, feed Grandmother. At times Damaris cannot fathom why she suggested this. There is something . . . *wrong* is not exactly the word . . . *off kilter* . . . what? The word does not come for what Damaris senses way down under the layers of duty and chores. Hardly a moment to think anymore, to know she's herself, Damaris Bishop and not Florence Nightingale; Cherry Ames, student nurse.

Most often the snow melts soon after falling, but in February it's cold enough for the snow to accumulate. The blacktop is icy and Damaris drives with extra caution, slow as an elder on the road. She feels slow all the time now, as if she swims against the current in the waters of Osprey Harbor, amid seaweed, amid jellyfish.

By March, Damaris feels she cannot continue, knows she must talk with Grand-pere, knows the nursing home is the solution. But she hesitates to make a firm decision, and while she hesitates, Grandmother makes the decision for them.

One night in mid-March, a strong, moisture-ridden wind rattles the windows. Overwhelmed by exhaustion, but unable to sleep, Damaris takes one of Grandmother's sleeping pills.

Around two A.M. she awakens. Groggy, dazed from the pills, she checks on Peter, at the foot of her bed. As usual, he has kicked his blanket to the bottom of his crib. She warms his pink toes in her hand, covers him once more.

The house creaks and shudders, the night light flickers. In the hall, a cold, moist draft billows her red-flannel nightgown.

In Grandmother's room, the blankets are thrown back; a damp spot marks where the old woman should now be sleeping.

Gone.

When she finds the front door open, Damaris awakens Pere, tells him to call the police. From the closet, she grabs Grandmother's gray-cashmere coat, thrusts her feet into Grandmother's fur-lined boots, and goes out into the night.

The road is empty. Uncertain where to search, she remembers a night long ago when Grandmother called Damaris's name as she hid by the scrub pine. Tonight beside the shed, Damaris calls to Grandmother over and over, calls and calls and, as in a nightmare, no one hears, no one answers.

By the time the rescue squad arrives, Damaris shivers, more from fear than from cold. "Lost," she tells the men.

Then she returns to the house.

"It's my fault. I should have slept in the same room with her . . . should have . . ." *Should have's*—too late now.

All night the police and volunteer firemen search the woods and the bogs, and well on into the morning.

"She is found." Horacio in the doorway. "In a bog near the highway."

They are seated at the table for a late breakfast when

Horacio arrives. The bowls of wheat flakes stand untouched except for Peter's. They all look up. Here is the answer: Found, but the question is . . .

"Alive when they found her," Horacio says. "Tucked in an old wooden shed . . . now in Falmouth Hospital."

Grand-pere and Damaris sigh with relief.

"Mama eat now?" Peter asks. Almost two, he speaks in short sentences, and Damaris's pride in him swells in the midst of her sorrow.

Tired and chilled, Horacio sits at the table, drinks a cup of tea, places his hand on Damaris's shoulder.

"The nursing home?" is all he asks, and Damaris nods.

"Folks don't realize, don't know, what they're into with this illness," Doc Wylie says later that day at the hospital.

"Can we see her?" Grand-pere asks, and they troop in and troop out in less than an hour. Grandmother sleeps, and when she awakens two days later she doesn't know them. Five days later she is transferred to the Mayflower Nursing Home.

"Promise you'll never put me in a nursing home," Grand-pere says. Solemn and morose, he sits hour after hour in his chair by the stove.

Damaris has no answer to that. It's not the sort of thing she would plan. Better to make no promise than to go back on it sometime.

"Story?" Peter asks Grand-pere, holding out *The Little Engine That Could,* his favorite. But though Pere takes the child onto his lap, it is Peter who "reads" to Grand-pere, points to the pictures with his stubby finger, giggles at the sight of the dancing bears, the milk bottles with eyes.

"Chug, chug," Peter says. "Toot, toot."

Several weeks after Grandmother enters the home, Grand-pere begins to visit. At first he stays but an hour, though soon he packs a sandwich and spends a good part of the afternoon, two or three days a week.

Peter returns to Agnes. Damaris returns to work. Tabitha Tobey, Cyrus Wing, Bertha North. "I'll hire you myself pretty soon," Jose says, for her arthritis has steadily gotten more debilitating.

April. A taste of warmth. On a chair in the front hall, Damaris sits behind the glass storm door in the soothing heat of the late-afternoon sun. Each afternoon when the sun reaches the tops of the trees across the road, Peter begins to fuss, Grandpere returns from the nursing home, dinner is in demand. But for a few minutes in between work and dinner, Damaris sits with Peter in her lap and they play Pat-a-Cake or Here Is the Church. Or she sits alone and, as Peter erects a block tower at her feet, breathes deeply, imagines another life. She'd be rich in the other life, with a nursemaid for Peter instead of Agnes, though Agnes is kind and caring. A housekeeper for chores, more time to spend in the shed with her shards.

In the evening after dinner, once Peter sleeps, Damaris retreats to the shed.

"No!" the child says when his mother announces the bedtime hour.

"Let's see who reaches the bedroom first," Damaris says, and she replaces the truck he clutches with a stuffed sock resembling a monkey. "One, two, three—go!"

Dressed in his footed pajamas, Peter laughs as he races, head forward like a turtle, feet slippery on the floor, monkey tucked beneath his arm. Damaris paces herself to allow him to win. Pillows at their backs, they lie on her bed for the story.

"Duck," Peter says. He hands her *Angus and the Ducks,* although he says "Agnes."

When they are settled, Peter dons his listening face: serious, lips pressed together, eyes squinting.

"Once there was . . ." she begins.

"Again!" he says, when she is finished.

"Once more, and then bed."

"Peter wants more story," he says later, once he's settled in the crib, now in Grandmother's old room.

"Good night," she says, winding his musical bear, ignoring his nightly plea.

"More."

Night light on.

"More."

Door ajar.

"More," he says, softer this time, and soon his voice fades as he hums along with the bear.

"Call me if he fusses," Damaris says to Grand-pere, as she heads out the door to the shed. Tabitha's Kleenex box cover gives her the idea. Not certain what might come of it, at first she plays with the shards. Italo invites her to search through piles of broken handblown glass heaped behind his shop and she combines those textures with the opaque shards of beach glass. On small sheets of clear glass, she attaches the shards with glue. The awkward, imperfect mosaics she devises line the shelves behind her. A waste of time, she often thinks, and yet she persists.

May. The new leaves on the tulip tree point upward, small green candles. Soon they will open into surprisingly broad, flat leaves. On Saturday morning, Damaris and Peter visit Grandmother. Peter wears his new spring corduroy jacket and a corduroy cap with an elastic strap under his pudgy chin.

"Oh, here he is, that dashing prince." As soon as Damaris opens the heavy glass doors of the Mayflower Nursing Home they begin: the nurses, the elders. They adore the child and whisk him away to the nurses' station, the recreation room.

While Peter entertains and is entertained, Damaris visits Grandmother, who sits alone in her room, unaware of who speaks. Doc Wylie says that it is good for Grandmother to hear a voice, like someone in a coma, and Damaris gets into the habit of talking to her in a way she had never done when the older woman could understand.

"I baked a carrot cake with cream-cheese icing for Peter's birthday. He blew both candles out, with a little help from Grand-pere, I might add. Logan sent money to buy him a wagon and a scooter. He wants Peter to visit Perth Isle this summer, but I said no. Two years old is too young to be away from his mother. . . ."

An hour later, when Peter returns to Damaris, a telltale rim of chocolate outlines his lips.

"Did you have candy?"

Too wise to be honest, too innocent to lie, he clamps his mouth shut, stares at his mother with innocent eyes.

"Candy?" the nurses repeat when Damaris inquires. Indignation resounds in their voices. "Not here. . . ."

"Candy?" The elders gathered round the television and the cribbage and beano tables. "Please, my dear . . . we know better . . . the very idea . . ."

Losing battle.

10

Fall 1969–Winter 1970

Although throughout the summer months Grand-pere continues to visit Grandmother with regularity, at home he remains quiet and withdrawn; not at all his usual gruff, outspoken self. Damaris worries.

"Depression, most likely," Doc Wylie says when Damaris telephones him with her concern. "Send him to me. I'll talk with him. Natural after something like this."

Grand-pere refuses. "Charge you an arm and a leg, and for what? Just leave me be, girl," he insists. "I'm fine."

But it is not until mid-August that Damaris feels confident he speaks the truth.

"So," he says one morning, as the three eat their breakfast of oatmeal pancakes and Vermont maple syrup. "Think it's about time you finished high school?"

"I can't go back now. I work. Besides, I'd be older than everyone else."

Grand-pere lifts his placemat and withdraws a rectangular clipping. "Says in the paper they're offering night classes toward completion of the diploma."

"Let's see." Three nights a week, from six to nine, she reads. "I'll think about it."

He taps the cutting with a hard, grainy nail. "Don't think too long. Registration's a week away."

From that moment on, Pere brings the topic up daily. "Made up your mind yet?"

"Don't want to set a bad example for this fella."

"Remember, you've got a built-in baby-sitter."

This one gives Damaris pause. Lately, Grand-pere's taken to walking with his cane. It's an old, old cane, carved by Grand-pere's father and varnished to a hard gloss, carved from a branch with alternate sections of dark brown bark and light wood where the bark had been removed. Damaris loves the cane, but the very fact that Grand-pere needs it makes her heart tremble.

On registration day, Damaris reads the list of classes: algebra, European history, typing. Non-credit courses are listed on the last page: knitting, Chinese cooking, creating a stained-glass window . . .

And her eye is caught. Stained glass? Recently her gluing projects have discouraged her. They end up looking clumsier than Tabitha Tobey's, and she has her blindness to blame. Who needs algebra anyway?

"Sometimes I think you were born with no brains. Sometimes I think they switched babies in the hospital and you belong to someone else, girl."

"I'm not a girl."

"Young lady."

"I'm a mother, a working woman, and—"

"And plain foolish . . . not an ounce of wisdom . . . just like your father. Bound and determined to do what you want, with no concern for anyone else . . ."

Damaris regards it as part of her slowly evolving maturity

that she does not answer Grand-pere back, contains her sharp retorts.

Sometimes.

The first night of class in September Damaris is surprised to see Myra Bea Rossiter, a girl from high school, standing at the worktable waiting for Mrs. Tyler to begin instruction.

"I remember you," Damaris says, going up to her. "You're the one who uses her middle initial as part of her name."

Myra Bea stares at Damaris from behind thick lenses.

"The B. What does it stand for?"

Myra Bea blinks her eyes from beneath long, black bangs in need of a trim. "Jeez!" she says, with a shout. "That's B-E-A! Beatrice . . . you know, after Dante's muse." She wears medieval-looking, round-toed clogs with "Birkenstock" etched in the leather. They look orthopedic to Damaris, who has a liking for canvas sneakers.

"You're the one who dropped out to have a baby? That true?"

Damaris nods.

"So. You have it?"

At school, some kids said Myra Bea was slightly retarded, so Damaris observes her closely through the weeks of the class. She is gruff, never bothered by speaking her mind, somewhat slow of movement and shy—in that, Damaris sees a reflection of herself—but hardly retarded. In fact, Damaris wonders if she might not be a sort of genius.

By the third week, Myra Bea has made an incredible glass picture the likes of which most of them can't complete after eight classes.

"Do you have a workshop at home?" Damaris asks her, envious.

"Library table."

Myra Bea lives with her parents in a twenty-room house

in Cataumet on a road labeled PRIVATE—RESIDENTS ONLY—POLICE-PATROLLED. Her parents don't allow her to live in the house proper, or so she claims.

"They say I'm a slob, but the truth is I didn't turn out like they wanted. You know, blond like you and tan and sportsy. Preppy, they call them. Special breed. Pink and green for women. Khaki and L. L. Bean boat moccasins for men."

Myra Bea wears a wool plaid kilt and matching vest in one of three colors: yellow, blue, or green. Because of her banishment, she lives in a large, three-room apartment attached to the main house, complete with a kitchen, bath, and water view.

Myra Bea reveals all this in the Mummichog Diner after class. At first, Damaris feels guilty about spending so much time away from Peter, but as Myra Bea reminds her, "The kid's asleep by now anyway, so you might as well live it up."

The Mummichog Diner is more of an outing than Damaris has had in some time. And so, after she telephones Grand-pere to ensure everything's all right, they order: a coffee fribble for Myra Bea, tea with lemon for Damaris. And they chat.

"Accidentally on purpose flunked the S.A.T. They say you can't flunk, but I did. Couldn't get into college. No need for that hogwash. Spewing the teacher's words back at her to get your Phi Beta Kappa key. Besides, one more poem by Thomas Gray and I'd have croaked. 'The curfew tolls the knell of parting day.' "

One thing about conversing with Myra Bea; Damaris doesn't have to talk much. A few "hmm's" and "oh, really's" are enough to keep Myra Bea going and to make Damaris feel a part of it all.

One day in October, Myra Bea invites Damaris to her home for luncheon.

"Eon, eon."

"Can Peter come?"

"Is he toilet-trained?"

"He does really well during the day."

"I don't know. . . ."

"It's not like having a puppy. He wears training pants."

"Okay. We'll try it and see."

The road turns to dirt as the blue station wagon passes between two stone pillars, as if entering a private estate, but in this case there are a number of private estates.

Beat-up as the station wagon is, Damaris hopes no one calls the cops, thinking she's a thief. She can hear some dignified, wary lady now. *Yes, officer, a girl and a midget dressed like a baby. They'll do anything to trick you nowadays.* The thought makes her laugh, and Peter, hearing her, laughs, too.

Damaris has never seen a house like the Rossiters'. Never close up, anyway. Never inside. She parks the blue wagon near the four-car garage and takes Peter by the hand. The driveway of crushed quahog shells is not easy walking for his two-and-a-half-year-old feet.

Damaris waits patiently on the porch for Peter to navigate the steps. Just as he reaches the top, Myra Bea whistles through her teeth and shouts "Over here!" from a door farther down.

In the spacious living room, two walls are lined with floor-to-ceiling bookshelves, some with double rows, some with stacks of papers and smaller books stuck in on top every which way.

A long mahogany library table holds Myra Bea's stained-glass materials. Scattered about in a disorganized manner are three saggy, overstuffed chairs. One chair holds a large dictionary, one a straw hat with a hole in it, and the third a cat reminiscent of Myra Bea, his eyes hidden behind bangs of fur.

"Kitty," Peter says, and he runs after the cat, scattering papers as he goes.

"Two more around here somewhere," Myra Bea says.

On the walls, old tapestries reach from ceiling to floor. Suddenly and quite sadly they remind Damaris of Logan's art. The memory leaves her queasy and dizzy for a moment. She rarely thinks of Logan anymore, stubbornly blocking him out of her everyday thoughts.

"Let's find Peter's ball," Damaris says when the child heads for a stack of books. By the time they find the ball in the sack of toys she carts with her everywhere, lunch is on.

In an alcove between the living room and kitchen, a small round table is set for three with mismatched china. Myra Bea is an excellent cook.

"Moussaka. Ever have it? Eggplant, tomato paste, cheese, and eggs. You wouldn't eat an animal, would you?"

Between mouthfuls, Myra Bea discusses the preservation of the salt marshes, one of her projects.

"There are more than four hundred kinds of insects in the salt marsh, and the land developers want to fill in . . ."

They are halfway through their moussaka when someone raps on the door. A thin, dark man in a shiny, threadbare, Grand-pere-type suit enters.

"Miss Rossiter invite your friends this afternoon. She say, invite tea?" He bows quickly and disappears. His woven-leather shoes make barely a whisper against the floor.

Damaris looks at Peter; Peter, balancing high on the dictionary, looks at Damaris. Neither says a word. Myra Bea continues chattering. "In 1962 the Jones Act was passed to protect the wetlands, and it said . . ."

Several hours later, the dishes stacked beside the sink, a tour of the yard and gardens complete, they head for the main house.

Hardwood floors scattered with Persian and American-

Indian carpets. Walls hung with masks of dark wood, shields and weavings "from Africa," Myra Bea whispers. Over the fireplace, hunting spears.

Mrs. Rossiter, tall and distinguished-looking, approaches in a ratty, V-neck cardigan with baggy pockets. She wears a hand-painted tie and smokes a cigarillo.

"Delighted," she says, offering her long, thin hand to Damaris, and Damaris, without thinking, goes through the left-hander's shuffle: extend left hand, pull back, offer the right, by which time Mrs. Rossiter has turned away.

In her wake follows Mr. Rossiter. Short and swarthy—for better or worse Myra Bea takes after him—he wears a white open-weave shirt and sandals like Myra Bea's.

"Pleased to meet you, Mr.—"

"Doctor," Myra Bea whispers in her ear.

"Dr. Rossiter."

"World-renowned archeologist," Myra Bea whispers again.

"World-renowned . . ." Damaris begins, then stops before she appears ridiculous. Hard to believe these two wanted a preppy daughter. Myra Bea must have been joking.

Peter heads for the tea cart set up before a round of chairs by the windows overlooking the water. Seated already are the gentleman in the shiny suit and two others who look much like him.

"Archeology students from Cairo . . ."

They are introduced, but Damaris cannot hear their names, feels overwhelmed, feels as if she's been hiding in a dark room with the shades drawn and suddenly a shade snaps up—in the way that shades do—and reveals . . .

Egypt, Africa, the fate of the fiddler crab, the periwinkle, shiny suits, narrow leather shoes, sandals with cork soles. She longs to draw the shade down again, to hide under the covers.

In spite of her worldliness, Mrs. Rossiter speaks only of

her daughter. Damaris holds Peter on her lap while he eats a scone, hears Mrs. Rossiter's words in sections.

"... pleased ... friend at last ... isolated ... otherworldly ... public school rather than private ... taste of the real ... discourage the esoteric ... still rather eccentric ..." Mrs. Rossiter grinds the cigarillo out in a large onyx ashtray in which the Egyptians have deposited the still-smoldering remains of strange brown cigarettes.

"... no doubt told you ... not allowed in main house ... but it is she who doesn't want to live here, not we who 'kicked her out,' as she is wont to declare. ..."

Myra Bea may take after her father in looks, but she takes after her mother in monologue.

Peter fusses. Overstimulation and the lack of his nap. He cries and Damaris jiggles him on her knees. "Trot-trot to Boston, trot-trot to Lynn ..." she whispers so as not to interrupt Mrs. Rossiter, but the child will not be distracted.

After a time, Damaris thanks Mrs. Rossiter, excuses herself. No one but Myra Bea notices when she rises to depart. The men are deep in conversation in a language Damaris has never heard.

"See you in class, Myra," she says. Myra Bea nods briefly from behind a blue scrim of smoke and allows her mother to escort Damaris to the door.

"Extremely pleased ..." Mrs. Rossiter continues, as she carries Peter's bag of toys and juice to the car.

"Especially as we travel so much ... off to Asia soon ... anything I can pick up for you there?"

Damaris is at a loss for words.

"Silk ... jade?"

"No ... no, thank you."

"Best get that one home for his nap. I remember this age. Quite the full-time job."

As Damaris drives away, she sees Mrs. Rossiter staring after the station wagon, her hands tucked into the puffy pockets of her sweater. Behind her, Myra Bea, a round, hunched shape, scurries off the porch, across the plush lawn, and over the shell-strewn path to her hideaway.

Once the stained-glass course begins, all Damaris thinks of is glass. By the end of the class in November, she has made a pretty good window. Even the teacher, Mrs. Tyler, thinks so. Twelve pieces of glass in variations of green.

"An abstract pattern," she tells Mrs. Tyler, though to Damaris it's the marsh grass, the way it ripples in the wind and changes colors. The picture seems a minor miracle. Whenever she feels down, she holds the small window up to her eyes and looks at the world through greens.

Now her sketchbook has purpose. She flips the pages through her early renderings of fruit and trees, through Peter's scribbles that look like illustrations of an atom's path. Plenty of blanks.

Throughout the winter, Damaris sketches. At first she copies drawings out of books, then later makes up her own. With or without Logan's help, she will learn to draw. A horseshoe-crab shell found on a beach walk becomes a model drawn over and over. She envisions a window, the crab in deep maroon-colored glass, the foreground bleached blond sand, touches of blue above.

New York. That's where Mrs. Tyler said supplies were to be found. Damaris has no idea how she'll get to New York, but one day she mentions her problem to Myra Bea.

"Write down what you want," Myra Bea says. "My parents are there all the time. They'll pick up what you need."

Money is the next question, but Damaris has been saving little by little, working extra hours. She has nearly enough money to lay in a good supply of glass and calme lead, to purchase the soldering iron and solder.

Tabitha Tobey, Cyrus Wing, Bertha North. Throughout the winter, Damaris tends to the old folks, and now Jose requests help two days a week due to her arthritis and Manuel's gout.

There's something about living in a world of elders. Something like: swollen joints and swollen feet, thinning hair and loosening teeth, fragile bones and faltering muscles; illness doing its slow creep like ivy—poison.

"And now, there's something wrong with Grand-pere," Damaris tells Grandmother.

It is early morning. Grand-pere stands in the kitchen, cup of tea in hand. Damaris rushes in, looks for Peter's winter jacket. She's late for Tabitha's and the old woman worries when Damaris is late.

"About ready?" she asks Pere, not even glancing at him, eyes focused on the crumpled blue jacket under the kitchen table.

"Third cup of tea," Pere says. "Usually only time for two."

Jacket in hand, Damaris crawls out from under the table and looks at him. "What's wrong with your shirt?"

"It's old, but respectable."

"It's on inside out," she says, in wonder. She inspects him closely. "And your belt is twisted, and your pants are unzipped." She sets down the jacket and helps Grand-pere straighten himself out. "You're as bad as Peter."

"Thinking on other things this morning, is all."

Several days later, Damaris observes Grand-pere moving a crossword puzzle back and forth in front of his eyes, as if to find the right distance for reading.

"Eye trouble?"

Startled, he drops the puzzle. "Nothing a good pair of glasses won't fix," he says, but his hand shakes, his cheeks flush.

Eye trouble. "I'll set up an appointment for you."

Retinal deterioration, the doctor says. Nothing to be done.

"Doctor's mistaken," Grand-pere insists. "Nothing wrong

with me," he says, but through the next months his vision worsens progressively.

"I'm afraid to let him drive anymore," Damaris explains to Grandmother, to prepare her for his less-frequent visits.

At first when Damaris puts her foot down about the driving, Grand-pere is not cooperative.

"What's that jangling?" Damaris asks, as he sneaks by her one afternoon.

"Loose change."

"Keys," she says, reaching into his pocket, in spite of his protestations. From then on she hides the keys in different places: an old tin in the pantry, under the crib mattress, in the bottom of the dirty clothes hamper. Half the time she can't recall where she put them and ends up checking all the hiding places herself.

They visit the nursing home together now and Damaris wonders if this will mean giving up her comforting monologues with Grandmother, but Grand-pere is restless. After five minutes or so, he makes his way to the recreation room, hand in hand with Peter.

As soon as the sound of Pere's cane tap-tapping against the linoleum fades, Damaris pries open a tin of horehound drops and sets to crunching and chatting.

"See this picture? Peter drew it and cut it out himself with a pair of blunt-edged scissors. Gotten clever with scissors. You may have noticed the patch clipped out of his bangs, by his own hand, mind you.

"He loves his Christmas present from Logan, a red tricycle with blue-and-white-plastic streamers on the handlebars. Of course, Logan sent the money and I picked it out. He rides up and down the driveway and round and about the schoolyard when I can take him.

"Logan has asked again for Peter to visit next summer, but I still think he's too young. He'll only be three. Better wait one more year, I wrote back. I don't want him to leave me, even for a few months, but Logan is so good, so faithful with his support. And Peter should know his father."

Grandmother shifts in her chair, tugs on the collar of her purple housedress that zippers up the front, smiles, and hums noisily.

Swollen joints and swollen feet, thinning hair and loosening teeth. Sometimes Damaris feels as if she is old, as if she's been born old, old in her mind, anyway. Already settled into tedious routine, routine that appears as if it will continue all her life with no break in the slow, daydreamy turtle rhythm.

If it wasn't for Myra Bea . . .

11

With the first hints of spring—purple crocuses pushing their way through the crusty soil, cats leaping as if tortured by a million fleas—renewed energy comes to Damaris. Sometimes she wonders if in another life she was born in a hot place like Cape Verde, she loves the warmth so, loves the sun, loves to sweat.

In April, she invites Myra Bea to visit the farm for a cleaning party.

"Yuk!" Myra Bea says, when she hears the word *cleaning*.

"I must confess to a great clumsiness in regard to cleaning houses."

What's a ten-letter word for "aversion"? *Clumsiness.* "Not the house, the shed. A matter of throwing out, painting, repairs."

"Why expend so much energy on a heap of a shed?"

"I plan to set up shop there."

"You don't strike me as the car-repair type."

"To work with . . . you know . . . the glass," Damaris mumbles, reluctantly revealing her vague intentions.

"Why didn't you say so to begin with? Would've saved all this lame-brained shilly-shallying. As my mother said when I was a kid, 'Give Myra Beatrice a hammer and nails and she's happy.' "

They set a date for the following Saturday. *Now,* Damaris thinks, *what sort of lunch will a vegetarian eat?*

Vegetarian . . .

"I should be delighted," Josiah Walters says, when Damaris asks for his help with the meal. According to Jose he's been feeling rather useless these days, having lost his part-time job at the North Osprey market.

On the Friday before cleaning day, Damaris and Peter meet with Josiah in Jose's kitchen for a cooking lesson.

"How's my boy?" Jose says to Peter, by way of greeting. Due to her arthritis, Jose spends much of the day in an easy chair, transferred from the living room to the kitchen. Beside her a small table holds a telephone, a pitcher of tea, and a transistor radio.

Josiah wears a white chef's apron. Brisk and efficient, he has arranged the counter with knives and bowls, flour and bulgar wheat, garlic and tomatoes.

"I'll keep it simple for your first lesson. . . ."

First lesson. Does he anticipate a vegetarian gourmet?

"Tabouli for the salad."

"Tabouli. That sounds like a good puzzle word."

"Easy as Jell-O. Simply place the bulgar wheat in a bowl and pour hot water on top."

"Me stir," Peter says, and Damaris hands him a wooden spoon, though his interest in cooking abates quickly.

While Peter drives his trucks along the floor among the many legs, including those of the table, Josiah and Damaris chop scallions and parsley, squeeze lemons, crush garlic, slice radishes. They mix whole-wheat flour, yeast, and water and knead the sticky dough into a loaf of bread for avocado, bean sprout, and tomato sandwiches.

"Some changes coming on," Jose says, while they work.

"Changes?"

"Connie Grouse is moving back to Ohio to live with her grand-niece, for one."

"And the other?" Damaris asks, as she opens the oven to bake the last dish, a pan of carob-almond brownies.

"With this arthritis, I can't tend to Manuel anymore. Got to send him to the home."

"Want me to come extra time for him?" Damaris has been tending to Manuel on the days she helps Jose; for the last four months he's been marooned upstairs in his bedroom due to his gout.

"We've already decided, me and the kids. I can't make it up and down those stairs but twice a day. It's too much."

"Are you closing the boardinghouse?"

"Just about, except for Josiah. He can tend to himself. In fact, he tends to me and Manuel now."

"Me thirsty," Peter says. While the brownies bake, they join Jose for a glass of iced tea; juice for Peter.

"Jacko wants some."

"Jacko?" Jose and Josiah ask in unison.

"Imaginary friend," Damaris whispers.

And a glass for Jacko is poured.

"Glad to see I'm not the only pack rat around," Myra Bea says, standing in the shed doorway at nine A.M. sharp the next day. She wears a pair of bibbed overalls, a plaid flannel shirt, and sneakers. This is the first time Damaris recalls seeing her out of her skirt, vest, and Birkenstocks.

"What a heap."

And so they begin. In boxes gathered at the North Osprey market, they pack broken saws and rusty nails, cans of crusted-over paint, oil-soaked rags, and stacks of dusty newspapers.

"These papers are old enough to be of historical interest," Myra Bea says, as she pauses to read an article.

"You're welcome to them."

"All I need's another pile of reading material," she says after a time, and dumps the lot. "We should get a Girl Scout badge for this. You ever a Girl Scout?"

"They'd never have the likes of me."

Myra Bea simply stares. "Likes of you? What's that mean?"

"You know. Dropout. Unmarried mother," Damaris says, almost whispering.

"So that's why you're such a shy, quiet thing. You've got nothing to be ashamed of. What you did millions of others have done through the centuries. Read history. Gives you some perspective. We think we're so important and we are, but we're just a few in a long line of millions, we're just tiny dots that hardly show up on the map."

"So you don't think it matters what we do with our lives?"

"I didn't say that. Would you listen? Of course it matters. But what matters is you do what's meaningful for you. Don't follow someone else's setup. Trample down your own path through the underbrush."

"Seems like most things I've tried so far haven't worked out very well."

"Nothing to feel glum about. Soon as one door closes, another opens. Well, look here. I don't believe I've seen so much beach glass in my life."

"Years' worth of collecting."

"Now, here's my point exemplified. To some, this'd be a heap of rubble."

"To Grand-pere, for instance."

"Litter washed up by the tide. But to your eyes it's—"

"Beautiful."

"Whatever. For you it's got something to say."

"I wouldn't go that far. It's just pretty."

"One man's garbage, another man's treasure. Which reminds me, the conservation commission is getting up a petition to promote a more rigorous wetlands protection act and . . ."

By lunchtime, they have loaded the back of the station wagon with cardboard cartons to take to the dump. They save only a few gardening tools, the lawn mower, Mitchell's lamp-working equipment.

At the kitchen table, Peter hammers nails into blocks of wood. "Me building a truck. Pa helped." Unable to say Grand-pere, Peter calls him Pa. "Next we'll paint."

"Next we'll clear the table for lunch."

"Pleased to meet you, sir," Myra Bea says to Grand-pere.

"Heard so much about you." Grand-pere squints and leans close. "The better to see you," he says. "Haven't seen overalls like those in years."

"All the rage."

"Pooh!" Peter says, when he tastes the green, mushy avocado sandwich.

"Don't spit out your food, child," Pere says.

"An acquired taste," Myra Bea says.

"How about peanut butter and jelly?" Damaris asks Peter.

"And while you're at it," Grand-pere says, "how about one for me?"

"You need to travel," Myra Bea says firmly. "Tangier. Zanzibar. Istanbul. Then you'd see what strange eating is."

"Just as happy not knowing," the old man says.

"This summer I'm vacationing in Peru. Sort of a vacation. I'll be studying the vegetation, too. And I fully intend to pick up some exotic recipes."

"A vacation. We haven't gone on a vacation in years."

"We live in the vacationland of the East Coast," Pere says. "For free."

"My lunch was a failure," Damaris says later to Myra Bea. In the shed once again, they scrub walls, dust shelves.

"There you go, silly girl. I thought it was delicious. Your grandfather will probably never come around to avocados and tabouli, too set in his ways. But you've got Peter started early enough."

"I envy you, Myra Bea. You've got such an interesting life. Your parents, your own apartment, your time open for you to do as you please. Like the vacation."

Myra Bea snorts. "Don't let appearances deceive. All of the above do not equal happiness. I envy you."

"Me?" Damaris has never imagined anyone would envy her.

"A secret love affair. A grandfather who loves you, a kid of your own. My folks don't care a hoot about anything but ancient remains. And I have yet to meet the man of my dreams. Besides that, you're pretty. A quality that's eluded me. I'm doomed to spinsterhood, I fear."

That afternoon and the next day they scrub and paint the walls a semi-gloss white. Myra Bea replaces the plastic window covering with glass. Jars of shards line the shelves, the asbestos-covered table has been dusted and cleaned, the old, blue cobbler's apron found in a drawer now hangs from a nail. Myra Bea has constructed a frame to hold the pieces of stained glass recently delivered by her parents from Bienenfeld's in Brooklyn, New York. The new soldering iron, glass cutters, and pliers await initiation. All is set.

The summer of 1970, colorful picture postcards from Peru cover the refrigerator door. Damaris takes the arrival of each new card from Myra Bea as an excuse to discuss the vacation she'd like, the vacation they deserve, the vacation . . .

"We can't afford . . ." Grand-pere says.

"I'll save," Damaris says. But try as she might, she cannot squeeze one more penny out of her meager income other than for daily expenses, with some extra for glass supplies.

Throughout the summer, Damaris and Peter don their thinking caps, fantasize about exotic journeys.

"Me first," Peter says.

"I'll start this time," Damaris says firmly.

"Why?"

Since he turned three, Peter's *why*'s beat a slow rhythm through the day. At times Damaris is tempted to ignore them, but usually she relents and answers.

"I'm the mother. I go first. Hmm. I want to see . . . Hawaii. The volcanoes, the brightly colored flowers. Your turn."

"Hmm," Peter says, imitating Damaris's tone. "Me want to see . . . the moon."

"That's one journey you'll take alone."

"Why?"

"And we're setting up something new for Grand-pere," Damaris says to her grandmother. "Starting in September he'll spend five days a week at the seniors center, while I work. It's a wonderful service. They pick him up in the van and . . ."

Damaris squirms in the rickety wooden folding chair provided for guests and looks carefully at Grandmother, looks to see what she is like in every wrinkle of her skin.

Once she figured Grandmother would be there forever in the kitchen, stewing prunes for breakfast, calling Grand-pere up from the basement workshop for a lunch of liver and onions.

Once she imagined Grandmother would flow quietly into a gentle old age, reminiscing about her life until everyone grew bored with the telling. Never in her dreams had she thought of anything like this.

"Ever since I came back from that island, things have been different," Damaris says.

Grandmother, propped up with pillows, nods. Sings: " 'Froggie went a-courting and he did ride . . .' "

"I'm closer to you and Grand-pere than ever before, and yet at the same time it's as if you're moving further away, as if you're on a ferry heading out and I'm standing on the dock waving."

" 'They all went sailing across the lake, mm-mm.' "

"I guess I was a handful for you. I guess it was hard bringing me up, old as you were. And now things have switched, now I'm the caretaker. . . ."

" 'They all went sailing across the lake,
And got swallowed up by a big, black snake, mm-mm.' "

October. Grand-pere is on a senior-citizens outing to the Mummichog Diner, where he absorbs sounds, smells, blurred sights, and "the best meal since Claire was cook."

Damaris stands at the asbestos-covered table wearing Mitchell's blue cobbler's apron. Since last April, when Myra Bea helped set up the shop, Damaris has been making windows. Today she works on her current project, panels of blue sky set against panels of green marsh grass, divided by creeks that twist and turn like dark blue veins. Ready, set, go. Three more shapes to cut and she can stretch the calme lead, lay the pieces out, ready to solder.

"You must concentrate, visualize the finished product," Mrs. Tyler had said in the stained-glass course, and Damaris tries, but today concentration eludes her.

She circles the table, gazes out the window. When she thrusts her hands into her pockets, she feels this month's check from Logan. He is loyal in his support for the child, and what does she give him in return? A brief letter now and then, reporting Peter's growth and antics.

Beyond the tulip tree, beyond Peter on the swing, the farmhouse appears abandoned. The windows are gray, unreflecting panels in the dim, squat body of the house.

"Jacko wants lunch," Peter says. Without her noticing, he's come up beside her.

"Me and Jacko rode the swing to Hawaii. Know what we saw? A whale. A great, huge whale. And it squirted water all over us, out of the hole in its head."

"That's how you got wet. I thought maybe the hose had something to do with it."

"Nope. That old whale is all. Right, Jacko?"

On one of those completely glorious days that occur on Cape Cod in November, Myra Bea arrives in her MG. To Myra Bea the car is special, but to Damaris it looks about as reliable as Grand-pere's station wagon—which isn't too—and much less handy for dump runs and groceries.

"I always expect one of those preppy characters to step out of this car. Not you."

"Incongruous, I know, but this is an *old* MG. Been through my dad and my mother before I ever got my hands on it."

"Doesn't that make it better? Being old, I mean?"

"For a high-school dropout you ask some pretty wiseass questions. Look, I brought us a picnic," Myra Bea says, pointing to an old-fashioned wooden picnic basket and a quilt. "Need company. My place is quiet as a tomb with my folks away. Soon as I returned from Peru, they took off for Cairo and beyond."

"I'll get Peter ready."

"Why not call the sitter? You need a break from that kid now and then."

Because of his eyes, it's difficult for Grand-pere to baby-sit now, so Damaris telephones Agnes. After they drop Peter off, Myra Bea hits the highway at top speed. Damaris braces her foot against the floor, grips the edge of her seat.

They drive to Sandy Neck; this time of year a deserted, windy strip of beach. Up one dune and down another they hike. The sun bakes hot against the sand, even on a mild day. A quick trip to the Sahara; the vacation Damaris longs for.

"Here's a good spot," Damaris says, though one spot looks like another in the dunes.

Myra Bea lifts a flat piece of driftwood out of the way and a mouse runs out and dashes up the hill.

"Who'd have thought a mouse would be out here?" Damaris asks, as she spreads out the quilt.

They weigh down the quilt ends with their shoes, though here they're protected from the wind. When she opens the picnic basket, Myra Bea reveals gazpacho made this morning, a loaf of rye, Havarti, yogurt, apples, and a Thermos of wine.

"What more can a body ask for?"

With her hand, Damaris shades her eyes from the bright, sharp light and watches a yellow-and-green kite dip and rise against the sky several dunes away. Today, with the whiz of sand in her ears, the faint hiss of the ocean beating its soothing chords, she feels free and easy, she feels as if she might soar with the wind.

"Ain't life wonderful," Myra Bea says, as she fills two cups with wine and hands one to Damaris. "My mother used to have conniptions when my grannie said *ain't,* which she did all the time, but I pointed out how it was classy to say *ain't* in the twenties. I quoted from Dorothy Sayers—you know her. No? Well, I quoted from one of her books where Lord Peter Wimsey says *ain't* throughout. I can't say it shut Mother up, but I do think it cut her back a bit. . . .

"Good thing you're so quiet or I'd never be able to go on so. . . . Have more wine and tell me what you're thinking."

Damaris gulps down the last of her wine and holds out her cup for seconds.

"I was wondering if there might be some other way for me to earn my living."

"You could go back to school. . . ."

Damaris makes a sour face. "I guess I'll have to some-day."

"Fantasize. In your wildest dreams, what would you do?"

"Visit all the churches in France with stained-glass windows."

"By the time you finished, you'd be ready for the nursing home."

"And I'd get lots of ideas and find me a bigger place to work in—the shed is cramped—and make stained-glass win-dows for people's front doors you know and maybe even for . . . oh, a hospital or a church. Years after I'm dead, folks will admire them."

"That's the longest speech you've ever made," Myra Bea says, as she pours the gazpacho into paper cups.

"It's the colors I love and how the glass catches the light. And the way looking through the glass changes the way the world appears. From dull to . . . to . . ."

"Delicious."

"That's not the word I'm looking for."

"The gazpacho. So how do you plan to go about making this fantasy real?"

"Crafts fairs. I've been thinking about this ever since Mrs. Tyler mentioned that's how she got started. We'll go together, you and me. Next summer."

"I only have about a dozen pieces."

"I have maybe twenty or so, but I'll work hard this winter. That'll be enough. Let's do it."

"I'm with you. Got to start somewhere, as they say."

"A toast to beginnings," Damaris says, and they raise their

cups together. "Just think, we'd never have met except for the class. Why did you take it, anyway?"

"So I could meet you. Never thought I'd meet anyone as weird as I am. An apple? Yogurt?"

Damaris takes a bite of apple, but she is not hungry. She stretches out in a semi-reclining position, leans her head on her arm. The sky against the sand is almost unbearable in its cold, clean line. What did she read somewhere? That if the earth were ever consumed with fire, maybe from bombs exploding all over the world as they did over Nagasaki and Hiroshima, then everything would fuse and turn to glass. Imagine, the whole world a huge sphere of glass.

"Do you ever wish you had a boyfriend, Myra Bea?" Damaris asks after awhile.

"Sometimes. Maybe that's why I travel so much. Figure I'll meet some sucker who doesn't know better. How about you?"

"Lately I've been thinking it'd be nice. But who? The boys my age seem like children after Logan."

"Whatever happened between you and that Logan fella? Why didn't you stick with him?"

"I have never told anyone this, Myra Bea, and I tell you only on the promise that you will never reveal a word."

"Oh, heck, yeah, I promise," Myra Bea says, as she opens a container of yogurt.

"Well, he almost killed Peter."

With her spoon in the air about to dive into the raspberry-flavored cultured milk, Myra Bea pauses. "No kidding. No wonder you left him."

"Yes, indeed." Damaris finishes her cup of wine, takes another bite of apple; her eyes begin to close.

"Hey, kid, wake up. You can't stop now at the good part. What did he do?"

"It was the baths."

"Baths?" Myra Bea sputters as she tries to suppress a laugh. "What'd he do, pop him in a tub of boiling water like a lobster?"

"This is serious. This is not funny. If you're going to laugh, I am not going to finish."

"Sorry. Go on."

"The cabin was drafty and cold, and Logan insisted on daily baths, and that's how Peter got pneumonia and almost died. It was Logan's fault."

Myra Bea ponders awhile, squishing her mouth this way and that, as if debating her response. "That's plain ridiculous."

"I am not diriculous."

"I have never heard anything so absurd in my life." Myra laughs.

"What kind of friend are you, anyway?"

"Maybe the drafts did do him harm," Myra Bea concedes, "but that's not the same as attempted murder."

Damaris pouts. "Maybe I am exag——exag——"

"Exaggerating?"

"Right."

"Hey, kid. I'm sorry. Truly, I am. You know what I think? You followed your intuition. Something made you leave that island and maybe you'll never figure out what, but whatever it was, I'm sure you did what you thought was best for you and the baby."

They sit in silence for a time. What Myra Bea says sounds true. Especially the part about never figuring it out. How does someone know for sure what draws them toward one person and not another? How does someone know what draws them away? For those answers Damaris must plunge to depths beyond her understanding, and once she plunges, how does she know the treasure she finds is anything but words?

The kite disappears, the sun changes position, the wind picks up.

"Should we think about heading home?" Myra Bea asks, but Damaris, who has been leaning on her arm, now collapses against the quilt.

"France," she whispers to herself, as she falls asleep.

"France."

12

Summer—1971

All through the winter and into the spring, Damaris laments their poverty, their provincialism. Peter is a companion in her daydreams—daydreams that become more exotic and sophisticated as time goes by.

In the atlas of the 1940 *Encyclopaedia Britannica* Grandpere bought long ago for Mitchell, they chart the routes of their fancy. Two blond heads bend over the page, two fingers arch to trace the names; to circle their favorites lightly in pencil. The Nile: Farriq–Kurusku–Aswan–Asyut. Madagascar: Manombo–Tamatave–Majunga. Greece: Trikhala–Domokos–Keos. On the Yangtze: Anking–Wuchang–Fowchow.

"Say Fowchow."

"Bow-wow."

"You're a silly. Say it right."

"Chowfow."

"Fowchow." But it takes a year's worth of laments before the vacation comes true.

On a morning in June, Damaris, still in her nightgown, gathers the dirty clothes for a load of laundry. From the bathroom, she hears the whir of the telephone dial. Peter, she thinks, is playing with the phone again, but when she enters the kitchen it is Grand-pere, requesting, of all things, a taxi.

"And just where do you think you're going all alone and nearly ninety years old?" she asks him, when he replaces the receiver.

"None of your nevermind," he says, and cane in hand, an ancient straw boater on his head, he makes his way slowly down the driveway to wait by the roadside.

Damaris runs into her bedroom, tucks her nightgown into a pair of jeans, and slips on a sweatshirt. She jams her feet into rubber thongs and drags Peter abruptly away from his wooden jigsaw puzzle. They make it to the curb as the taxi arrives.

"Hyannis Bank and Trust," Grand-pere tells the driver, and with Grand-pere in the front seat, Damaris and Peter in the rear, the taxicab carries them out of the village, through the heart of the Cape and into Hyannis.

"Why is that man driving?" Peter asks, still clutching a camel-shaped puzzle piece in his hand.

"I'll drive you anywhere you want," Damaris says, ignoring the child for once. "You know that. You just have to tell me."

"Didn't intend to have company this trip."

When they arrive at the bank, Grand-pere requests that the taxi wait, orders Damaris and Peter to remain in the car.

"Crusty old man," Damaris says out loud, and she would have said more, but the cab driver gives her such a look that she feels ashamed. And what does he know of tending to old men? Grand-pere might fall or forget where he is, although *his* memory's pretty much intact.

Taking Peter by the hand, Damaris paces up and down the sidewalk, peers through the bank window. No sign of Grand-pere, only her own foolish reflection. A skinny, blond woman with a nightgown bunched up around her waist and likely to fall down around her knees at any moment.

At last, Grand-pere comes out of the bank, and without a word they travel home again. When they're in the kitchen once more he throws an envelope onto the table.

"Your dowry." And other than telling her it's for a vacation, that's all he says about the money.

The old blue station wagon sputters and puffs its complaint against the humid lethargy of the air. The black tar hums a lullaby beneath them. Damaris grips the wheel tightly, tired in spite of something like ten cups of tea. They are heading for a lake in upstate New Hampshire to spend a few days in the Rossiters's summer cabin. An ordinary, peaceful family vacation; not exotic at all.

"Darned traffic," Damaris says, more to herself than to anyone in particular.

Four-year-old Peter squirms on the tattered seat beside her, a Donald Duck comic book draped over his dry-skinned knees. He peers at his mother as if to say, "You're the one who insisted on this vacation."

After four days at the lake, they will rendezvous in Fairweather Harbor with Logan; Peter will spend the rest of the summer on Perth Isle. Logan has asked a number of times, and much as it sorrows Damaris to part from the child, it seems a good idea for Peter to know his father. "A man's touch," as Miss Winnie said. Damaris knows what it's like to be without a father.

Summer on the island, she reasons, will not be as harsh as that dreadful winter, and improvements have been made, Logan assures her.

"You never know, this may be our last vacation together," Damaris says to Peter.

"Our last" is not exactly what she means. Grand-pere's

last is more like it. Through the rearview mirror she sees Grand-pere in the backseat, his eyes closed, his chin on his chest, his hands resting on the curved wooden handle of the cane between his knees.

"Hand me my barrette, please," Damaris says, pointing to the glove box, when a wisp of hair blows into her eyes.

Peter hands her the silver clip and she releases the wheel to fasten her thin, yellow hair away from her face. The car wavers and weaves, crosses into the other lane, then back, brushing the sandy shoulder.

"Let's go the back way," Damaris says. She smiles at Peter. His hair, pale as moonlight, hangs in his eyes. Mitchell's spitting image, Grand-pere says. None of Logan's darkness.

As they turn off the highway onto the narrow, curved road, Damaris relaxes her grip on the wheel and sings. Driving and singing give her that light feeling she had when she was young and played on the backyard swing, going higher and higher, the air rushing against her, her dress blowing, her legs pumping, singing then, too, as loud as she could. It hadn't mattered that she was off key.

They arrive at the lake in the late afternoon.

"The Pearly Gates?" Grand-pere asks, waking when she hits the bumpy dirt road to the cabin. "Are we there?"

Stiff from the journey, he leans against Damaris as she leads him into the cabin. Once inside the high-ceilinged living room, she opens two doors that form a wall facing the lake and the wall becomes a wide-screened window.

"I could stand here forever," she says, as she smells the fresh water, the pines.

"Stomach's growling," Grand-pere says, resting on his cane beside her.

She sighs. Crusty old man.

Later, as she opens a can of soup, Peter races past with his sand toys and trucks.

"Remember," she says, as he slams out the door, "no swimming unless I'm there to watch."

At a small table in front of the screened living room window, Grand-pere sips noodle soup, Damaris drinks tea. Outside, Peter launches into a series of creaks and *brrmm*'s, his truck imitation.

"Won't be long now," Grand-pere says.

"Nope. Not much time left for that old car." She knows he doesn't mean the car.

"Be grown into bigger britches soon, that one. Won't even grudgingly vacation with us," he says, as he stirs his cooling soup.

"Hush. He's only four." She doesn't want to think of the changes ahead. No sense worrying about the child's teenaged years yet.

"Where will you live when he's grown?"

"Where I live now, of course. We can rent his room to an aging woman for you," she says, then regrets her lack of sensitivity. The truth is, they visit Grandmother less often these days, and the older woman slips out of Damaris's everyday thoughts.

"Ain't me that's in need of that." He shoves his soup bowl to the center of the table. "We aren't meant to journey alone," he says.

"We won't journey at all if I don't fix that wobbly exhaust pipe."

"Look at the stars. Far apart as they are they have companions, join with their kind. Look at the patterns they make."

"Ten years is a good stretch for a car."

"You've been hanging out with us old-timers way too long."

"I like old-timers."

"Ah, well," Grand-pere says, rapping his fingers against the table. "What do I know? I'm just an old man."

The next day, in a spot of late-afternoon sun, Grand-pere sits in a redwood lawn chair padded with cushions. At his feet, Damaris and Peter lounge on the sandy lawn bordered by clusters of black-eyed Susans and white daisies.

"When I was a girl, I used to weave chains of daisies to wear on my head like a crown. Kids don't have that sort of fun anymore," she says to the boy, bent over his comic. A sense of mischief overcomes her and she braids a daisy into Peter's yellow hair.

Drawn away from the roadrunner's antics at last, Peter swats the flower, and when it fails to dislodge, he pulls it out and loops the stem into a loose knot. Nonchalantly he strolls behind his great-grandfather.

"Ready, aim, fire!" he shouts, drawing the stem back like a bowstring.

The flower pops into the air and hits Grand-pere on the side of his head. The old man stands with difficulty, raises his fists. "Put up your dukes, sonny," he says, squinting, peering around for the child. Even a year ago he was more agile, his vision sharper.

"Beat you to a pulp!" Peter shouts, as he skitters around Grand-pere, raises dust, wrestling with the old man as Damaris did when she was a child.

"You young folks got no respect," Grand-pere says, buffing Peter on the arm. As he moves about, his long, white hair falls out of the single braid Damaris weaves for him each morning when she should be doing other things.

"This is baby stuff," Peter whispers to his mother. He pretend-fights to make Grand-pere happy, but it's no fun anymore.

———

With a rusty coffee tin, Damaris bails water from the bottom of the rowboat, then helps Grand-pere into the prow. Even before they set out, he grips the seat with both hands, as if expecting a speed-boat ride.

"All aboard that's coming aboard," Damaris says, and Peter settles into the stern with a can of worms and a fishing pole.

Damaris eases the splintered, green oars into the oarlocks, dips the flat, wooden paddles into the lake. The water is smooth and calm; branches of maples and pines grope into the blue sky.

"What a nice lake," she says, as they slowly traverse the shoreline, past a group of summer cabins.

"I wish Claire were here to enjoy this," Grand-pere says, and with these words Damaris misses her, too, misses her simple, uncomplicated love. She can see why they stayed married so long, those two. Grandmother's nature balanced his; they melded together in flavorful contrast, like a sweet-and-sour Chinese dinner.

"If it weren't for Grandmother . . ." she says, quietly to herself, remembering how the old woman was her mainstay of support through those hard years when Grand-pere rejected her.

"What are you harping on now?" Grand-pere says.

"Never mind." Nothing wrong with his ears.

"Might as well out with it."

"Fish are jumping," she says, pointing to the ripples on the water's surface ahead.

"Oh, boy!" Peter says, and he drops his baited line over the side of the boat.

"You and I view the lake from different shores. Always have, always will," Grand-pere says.

"You can love someone you don't see eye to eye with," she says, hinting for an admission of caring on his part.

Grand-pere sighs and slumps in his seat. "I'm no good for anything nowadays."

She shouldn't have said that about seeing eye to eye.

"Might as well be dead."

"Don't say such things in front of the baby."

"Baby? I'm four."

"And well I remember when you were born. Grand-pere refused to drive me to the hospital."

"Didn't have the chance. The women took over."

"That's not the way I remember it." Why is she on to this? It won't get her anywhere. Maybe it doesn't even matter. So long ago.

Grand-pere closes his eyes and pouts. "No good to anyone anymore."

"Shh!" Peter says, finger to his lips. "The fish."

"That's it, boy," Grand-pere says. Lively once again, he punches the child lightly on the arm as if they are conspirators. "Keep your mother in line."

"It's not just me . . ."

"Stop!" Peter shouts. His voice echoes across the lake.

Pathetic, Damaris thinks. Two adults brought to task by a child. Sometimes it seems as if they're poison to each other, Grand-pere and Damaris. Can't sit together for more than ten minutes without finding something to disagree about.

"Ah, well," Grand-pere says, sighing.

"What do I know? . . ." Damaris adds.

"I'm just an old man," they say, in a harmonious trio.

They row among the lily pads and reeds until night moves in and the sky becomes light behind the darkening trees. Everything appears twice; the real trees and their reflection in the water form a new shape. Just as when Damaris used to write her name in crayon, fold the paper, and rub, and new letters appeared; upside-down shadows of the ones she wrote.

At two in the morning, Damaris wanders through the cabin, shivers in a long summer nightgown. She pauses in Grandpere's doorway. His cane is hooked on the bedpost. He snores restlessly. In the next room, Peter sleeps with arms spread wide across the bed; one leg hangs over the side of the mattress, the covers twist around the other. When she unwinds the sheet he moans, sits, opens his eyes.

"Shh!" she says, and clasps his shoulders, moving him to her. Soon they will be parted for the first time. Peter circles her waist with his arms and rests his head on her chest. A deep feeling stirs in her for a moment: the memory of a baby, head in the crook of her arm, soft fuzz of hair against her skin. As the memory settles like a particle of sand to the bottom of the lake, she closes her eyes, tries to reach that place once again, but there is only the hushed whisper of the warm night wind and the rhythmical breathing of the child, asleep once again.

13

Several days later, they drive to Fairweather Harbor. As they turn into the parking area at the ferry terminal Damaris spots Logan standing in the sun, gazing out over the water.

She parks, turns off the engine, breathes deeply. For days she has said farewell to Peter in her mind, releasing him to explore a broader world than she had known as a child. For days she has dreaded seeing Logan, wonders if his longing for the child may evoke further pleas for her return to the island.

"Want to stretch your legs, Grand-pere?" Damaris asks, as she opens her door, crosses to the passenger's side.

"Fine right here," Grand-pere says from the backseat.

Grand-pere has been subdued lately, faded and withdrawn. Maybe the trip has been to hard on him. Maybe he's too old and fragile for such a long expedition. As Damaris helps Peter out of the car, Logan approaches.

Lean. Logan has remained lean. His shiny black hair is long now, worn in a single braid down his back, like Pere's.

Peter, his red-canvas sneakers set firmly on the ground,

stares at Logan, then clings to Damaris, hides his face in her skirt.

"It's Logan, your dad." Her ankles feel weak, her feet as unsteady as if she wears ice skates for the first time. It's been a long drive.

"Take time for him to know me. Like before," Logan says. "Why don't we walk down to the luncheonette? Have a bite."

Reluctantly, Grand-pere emerges from his hideout. Leaning on his cane, he squints at Logan from beneath his straw boater.

"Yep. I recall you, son. I tried to picture you for the longest time. Now I know."

In the restaurant, a wooden ceiling fan turns in waltz time. Grand-pere, Damaris, and Peter crowd into one side of a booth; Logan sits alone on the other.

When they're apart, she rarely thinks of Logan except for brief flickers of wonderings that rise up now and then. Had she been foolish? First to imagine she loved him; second, to leave him?

"Billy Flynn's got a litter of golden retrievers, Peter. You can choose one for your own."

Peter's face brightens with excitement. "A puppy!"

The child looks at Damaris, a question in his eyes.

"For the summer only," she says. "No puppy in our house. Not with . . ." She nods her head several times in Grand-pere's direction.

"I saw that," Grand-pere says. "I'm not totally blind."

That's the old, feisty Grand-pere.

"I'm not the one that's got a problem with dogs." He nods in Damaris's direction.

They order fried clam rolls—Damaris and Logan; and hamburgers—Peter and Grand-pere. But when the clam rolls arrive, Damaris takes two bites and no more, her stomach jostled from the drive.

"Full," she says, placing the roll on Logan's plate.

"I want clams," Peter says.

"Open your mouth and close your eyes and I'll give you a big surprise."

Peter giggles, scrunches his eyes shut, and Damaris dangles a clam above his open mouth like a mother robin with a worm.

"Mm-mm. My friend Jacko likes clams," Peter says. "And dogs."

"Jacko?" Logan asks.

"Imagination," Damaris whispers, hand beside her mouth so Peter won't hear.

"Jacko's coming, too," Peter says.

"And where will Jacko sleep?"

"With me. He sleeps with me."

"I want to let you know," Logan says to Damaris, "Peter and Jacko and I will be taking a trip to visit an old friend in Canada. A weaver. Cards wool from her own sheep. I'm thinking of buying sheep for the island and . . ."

Her? Somehow, in Damaris's claustrophobic mind, she has never envisioned Logan with a *her*. Damaris holds a picture of Logan tramping the terrain of his rocky island alone, not gallivanting off to see friends in Canada. A shepherdess, at that.

"How about you?" he is saying to Damaris. "Any romance in your life?"

Damaris opens her mouth to speak, but she halts at the sound of Grand-pere's voice.

"Dry as a bone," Grand-pere says, sotto voce.

Damaris opens her mouth wide in astonishment, though heaven knows she should be used to it by now.

"Ice cream," Peter says, pointing to the giant cone hanging over the counter by the door, saving his mother from the need to respond. "I want vanilla."

"Come with me," Logan says, and he holds out his hand

to the boy. Peter glances at his mother as if he senses parting is some sort of betrayal, but Damaris nods and he is gone.

At one, the ferry departs. "Love you, and have fun," Damaris says, crouching to draw the boy to her, hugging him tightly.

"Love you, Mom," he says, and his lips print a moist outline against her cheek.

"Love you," she repeats, when he climbs the ramp to the deck. She waves, her skin warm from holding his small frame, waves until she can no longer see the child. *It is only until September, it is for the best, it is good for the child to know his father.* These are the words she repeats to herself, to give herself comfort.

As soon as they return to North Osprey on Sunday evening, Damaris telephones Myra Bea.

"So, how did it feel to see that man again?"

"It was hard letting Peter go."

"I wasn't talking about Peter."

"I don't know." Myra Bea always wants answers *now;* sometimes it takes Damaris years to figure out what she feels.

"I could never live on Perth Isle now. Even with the improvements there's no power for the soldering iron."

"Speaking of soldering, I reserved a table for our first crafts fair in Cataumet. July 15, so follow the Girl Scout motto."

"Girl Scout motto?"

"Be prepared."

Damaris is prepared. Since last November, when they spoke of displaying their wares at crafts shows, she has completed one small window a week. Wrapped in newspaper and stacked in cardboard boxes, they await their time to be revealed to the world.

On Monday morning, Damaris stirs oatmeal atop the wood-fired cookstove. Today the cereal is gooey, not to mention ridiculous fare for June, almost July, but Grand-pere insists.

"Keeps me regular," he tells her.

As she tosses in a handful of raisins, he appears in the doorway.

"How do I look?"

Disheveled as a two-year-old trying to dress by himself, she thinks, setting the wooden spoon on the Florida spoon rest.

"You won't make the men's fashion supplement."

"I feel out of line somehow. Lopsided."

She sighs and rebuttons the green-cotton shirt, rolls trousers cuffs down and socks up, ties laces. "Got your handkerchief?"

"Feel queasy this morning," he says, as he takes his chair. "Indigestion."

She dishes the oatmeal into a bowl and sets it before him on the table. "Last night's hot dogs and beans, most likely."

He covers the mound of hot oats with three spoonfuls of brown sugar and nibbles small portions.

"Not much longer for this world," he mutters, and shakes his head.

"Why don't you come with me to Jose's today?" Damaris knows he dislikes going to the seniors center so often, but he can't stay alone while she works, not anymore.

"Nah. Just be in the way."

After breakfast she combs and braids his hair, gives him his dollar for lunch, and by the time the van arrives at ten he seems less distressed.

Over the past year, Jose's arthritis has advanced to the stage where she's stooped to half her size, and she was small enough to begin with.

"At last, here you are, here you are," Jose says from her bed in the converted pantry; she can no longer navigate the stairs. Divested of shelves and cupboards, the room provides barely enough space for the narrow twin bed, but Jose refuses to sleep in the parlor. Only those on death's door sleep in the parlor.

Damaris, crammed awkwardly between bed and wall, puts an arm around the crippled woman as she slowly eases her legs to the floor. On twisted feet, Jose hobbles to the bathroom, recently installed in a cramped closet under the stairway. Some mornings the old woman moves about on legs so unsteady Damaris wonders if she's been guzzling elderberry wine.

The arthritis prevents Jose from doing certain chores, so Damaris cooks her a late breakfast, opens a jar of pickles, peels potatoes and carrots. Later, she continues the job begun last month: clearing out the closets. And there are many. Since her affliction, Jose's fanaticism with cleaning has gone by the wayside. Although Damaris does her best, her work cannot compare with the immaculate, cobweb-free spotlessness Jose once maintained.

According to Jose, the closet clean-out is to prepare for her death or the nursing home, whichever comes first.

"I'd rather die," she says. "Look what happened when Manuel entered the home. He turned bitter and forgetful," she repeats often, as if to confirm the logic of her preference.

Today, Damaris begins on Miss Winnie's old room. The cleaning is a tiresome two-step procedure. She fills cardboard cartons, carries them downstairs, displays each item to Jose like a salesperson demonstrating wares. The wares go into one of three piles: keep; children; Salvation Army.

Six cartons are full when she finds the forgotten boxes of Miss Winnie's poems tucked behind a stack of books in the back of the closet. Hundreds of pages, smelling faintly of roses, stuffed carelessly in boxes that once contained shoes: Life Stride, Matrix, Vitality, Red Cross.

Crouched on the floor, she begins to read. Lines leap out at her, lines that sound familiar, lines Miss Winnie once quoted.

> As daylight rolls under
> earth's rim and
> long, magenta clouds fade,
> we rise from rocks dark as
> wet kelp. Forgotten
> memories rise too
> as we yearn for times lost.

Absorbed, Damaris forgets where she is.

"Jose says to tell you doomsday will come first. . . ." Josiah says, coming up behind her.

"Doomsday?" she repeats, startled by his sudden appearance. Blinking to refocus her eyes, she gazes up at him.

"Indeed. Doomsday will arrive before you make it downstairs with the boxes. Just repeating her very words."

"Be there in a minute," Damaris says, returning to the pages, forgetting his message as soon as he departs.

It's Miss Winnie's life the pages depict. The pattern of her years from youth to old age, delineated in verse. A number of pages are stapled together like a book. "The Bishop Poems," the title page says. Are they religious? Or had Damaris inspired the bard to write new verses in her old age?

"With much love to Franklin Bishop," the dedication reads. Franklin Bishop? Appearing to be written for the child's father, the poems tell of Miss Winnie's love affair, pregnancy, and all that followed.

> If you would but return
> to me
> I would bow

I would place tea roses at your knees
I would let blood from the nearest vein.
You do this too.

Let us touch wrist to wrist.
Let us vow consonance.
Let us risk devotion.
Let us be kind.

But Grand-pere couldn't be involved; he couldn't be the father. If that were true, Miss Winnie would have let on that she once loved the crusty old man. If that were true, Grand-pere would never have been so unbending with Damaris.

Before she has time to absorb the matter further, Jose clangs her bell for attention. Damaris crams the poems into the shoeboxes and stomps down the stairs with a cardboard carton full of linens.

"What have you been up to all this time?"

"Drawers and closet are bare as a bone," Damaris says, dropping the carton onto the floor with a thump.

"Thought maybe you found some fellow up there I didn't know about."

"Don't start on me, Jose," she says, more sharply than she intends. Always trying to fix her up with some man or other, as if a man alone can salve life's loneliness.

"You look like you swallowed a fly."

"More like a wasp."

"Talk to me."

But Damaris stomps out of the room, in and out six times with six cartons.

"Now that that's done, set yourself down—and that's an order."

Damaris places a stack of yellowed sheets and pillowcases on the table. "We'd better sort or we'll be here till midnight."

"Take the lot to the Salvation Army," Jose says, waving her hand in a grand dismissal.

"There's some good stuff here!"

"Come on, now. Get it off your chest."

"Agnes might want this." Damaris holds up a pillowcase monogrammed with an "S" for Santos.

"She's been a Barrows since she married that no-good husband of hers. Now don't change the subject again. Don't you trust me? After all we've been through?"

Damaris sits and rests her chin against the smooth sheets stacked before her. "Some things need to be kept in the family."

"You found *your* skeleton in *my* closet?"

In spite of herself, Damaris smiles at the joke. She imagines it's true every family has some sort of secret or other. Here she spent years thinking she was the black sheep, guilty for disgracing the family, and all along Grand-pere . . . well . . . no sense getting agitated. It's not the end. . . .

". . . end of the world," Jose drones on. "You'll survive, whatever it is. You're a survivor."

And now Damaris makes a firm decision. She'll confront Grand-pere with the poems. Make him account for himself. It might cause a rift when things had calmed between them, but she can't let this pass. She must know. For once, she will take things in hand. For once, she will shape circumstances and not let circumstances roll over her, shaping her in their wake. Suddenly she remembers Grand-pere pushing a big, metal, water-filled grass roller to flatten the lawn. Things are about to change; now she will do the pushing.

At that moment, the telephone by Jose's elbow rings.

"Santos's residence. . . . Yup. She's here."

Damaris lifts her head, alert now. Peter? Something's happened to Peter?

"Yup, yup." Jose covers the speaker with her hand and mouths "Pansy Whitcomb from the seniors center."

"I'll tell her. Now when . . . I'll send her along."

It's Grand-pere. That's the only reason Pansy Whitcomb would call. Something's happened.

"They brought him to Falmouth Hospital," Jose says. "He just sort of flopped over."

14

When Damaris first learned to drive she would hit the highway with such anxiety that the trees lining the route, the
occasional glimpses of the bay and cranberry bogs, might as
well have been the moist, mustardy walls of the Callahan
Tunnel for all she noticed them. Eventually, this tunnel vision
faded in proportion to the fading of her anxiety. Today,
however, she sees only the black tar broken by flashes of
yellow.

Every time Damaris enters a hospital, she recalls Peter's brush
with death. The atmosphere makes her shiver, all the concrete
and hush and whisper; everyone so cold, efficient, and busy.

In room 202, aluminum bars protect both sides of the bed.
Grand-pere lies as if in a coma, eyes closed, still. His arm is
blue from failed attempts to insert the IV needle, which now
enters a vein below his inner elbow.

In a chair beside the bed, Damaris waits for him to open
his eyes; when she sees his eyes she'll know he's all right. The
palm of her hand presses against his knuckles. In earlier years,
his hands had been raw and chapped from chopping wood

in the winter cold. When he play-boxed with her, his knuckles would raise like red welts, the knobby bones prominent. Today, his hands are pale, fragile, the skin almost translucent, the bones as thin and delicate as a mole's.

For several days Grand-pere remains unconscious. Damaris cancels her home-care clients once again. She telephones Mrs. Twine at the Haven Inn, asks her to have Logan call her when he picks up his mail. In spite of a need to see Peter, Damaris agrees with Logan that it's best for the boy to remain on the island unless things change for the worse. There is not much Peter can do for Grand-pere; a child so young would only be in the way.

For years Damaris and Grand-pere bickered and she prayed he would remain silent. Now, suddenly he's mute and she prays he'll speak. She knows so little, about his life, bits and pieces picked up here and there that fade as soon as they're spoken.

Now there are two who can't speak: two who remain silent, two who hold their history within. Damaris visits Grand-mother for the first time since the vacation, talks in soothing tones. Sometimes Grandmother smiles and nods, appears to understand, appears to be content to listen, though Doc Wylie claims her comprehension remains almost nil.

"You must have loved Grand-pere very much to put up with his shenanigans," Damaris says, thinking of the poems. "Did you ever falter? Did you ever wonder if it was not love, but habit, that kept you together? Maybe in your day such wonderings weren't voiced or even thought."

Damaris once thought love a solid thing; what Grand-pere and Grandmother had together. And Twyla and Mitchell. But now, she thinks love has about it the quality of glass. Glass appears solid, but this is deceptive, for glass is a liquid; it flows and expands with heat, freezes and contracts with cold, it has the ability to sag.

And so love. For love sags in the heat of betrayals and infidelities; withdraws in the frigid temperature of a frozen heart.

Grandmother smiles a toothless smile. Her dentures have lost their ability to chew and to charm. The old woman cocks her head as if to ask a question, reaches up the sleeve of her sweater, withdraws a handkerchief embroidered with a blue "C," and offers it to Damaris. It is only then that Damaris feels tears gathering in the curve of her lips.

Three days after his hospitalization, Grand-pere opens his eyes. Damaris holds her breath for fear it's an illusion. His skin is pale, his eyes bloodshot, but open. The yellow-stained catheter bag sways as she lowers the bed bar to bend near, kiss his gray cheek, prickly from lack of shaving.

Several days later, his bed raised, he sucks down cubes of Jell-O. Stroke is the diagnosis. His left side is somewhat paralyzed, speech is difficult. Nothing to be done.

Gradually, he advances from broth to more substantial foods, gradually the paralysis lessens. Doc Wylie says Grand-pere might continue like this for months, might even improve, and so, after two weeks, Grand-pere returns home; bedridden, but home.

Certainly Damaris can't complain of not being prepared; her experience will do her in good stead. He rests, a faded man against the faded sheets, sheets oversized for the hospital bed borrowed from the nurses' association. A bell for him to ring when he needs her stands on his bedside table. A paper bag hangs from the bed bar for his refuse.

At first, he sleeps much of the time; cannot be left alone for long. Once more, Damaris quits her job, uses his Social Security check to get by.

"You rang?"

"Urinal's full." He hands her the plastic container.

"Hottest July in history," she says. "Want a fan?"

"Mostly I'm cold."

With time on her hands, Damaris is restless. No job to rush to, no child to tend; restless but exhausted. The old man wakes her in the night.

"You rang?"

"Bedpan."

She slides the pan under him, covers him lightly with the sheet, prepares the wet washcloth. Absolute, impeccable cleanliness prevents bedsores.

"Sit by me, girl." She obeys. Holds his hand through the rail. Reads to him the way he read to her when she was a child, though he doesn't often listen to the words.

"It's the quiet hum of your voice I like," he says.

Some days he's stronger than others and she lowers the bed, lets him dangle his legs over the side. Some days she holds his arm while he plods to the bathroom.

"Cheer up," he says on these days when he sees beyond himself. "You seem unhappy."

"Were you happy with your life?"

"From this bed everything looks different. Smaller. Things that mattered don't matter anymore."

He loses five pounds, then five more on his eternal cups of broth and toast; no appetite, like Miss Winnie at the last.

"I read a psalm with Miss Winnie when she was sick. 'The Lord is my shepherd.' Want me to look it up?"

"Don't need any psalms."

This is as close as she's come to approaching the subject of Miss Winnie. Several times she's reread the poems, and if they reflect the truth, there's no question of Grand-pere's involvement. She's practiced various openings over and over:

"How did you come to know Miss Winnie?"

"Why didn't you tell me about my half-aunt?"

But whenever she approaches speaking out, she falters. His strength rarely lasts long and sometimes she's relieved when he fades into sleep before she can speak. Maybe she should burn the poems, scorch them out of her head and heart. Does it matter now? How can she be furious with a dying man?

Every now and then as Grand-pere sleeps, Damaris drags her feet across the grass to the shed. Not with any real purpose toward distraction or completion; she simply sits down at the kitchen table for a tea break and moments later finds herself at the workbench pressing the cutter with a delicate touch into rectangles of colored glass.

For the current project, orange, brown, white, and ocher panels are juxtaposed, using paint-by-numbers contrasts, to form a face; the aged, lined face of a man. At first, Damaris thought to do a portrait of Grand-pere, but as she worked, the portrait evolved into someone unknown, an almost mythical ancient.

After discussion with Myra Bea, they cancel their crafts-fair plans and Damaris reluctantly releases her vision of extra earnings for this summer. She progresses slowly now, only half concentrates, ready to run if Grand-pere signals her with the bell she's rigged up to a wire pulley.

On one of Pere's good days, she sits by the bed and reads a few of Miss Winnie's poems aloud; she's decided a tiff might draw the life back into him. Beginning with innocuous nature poems, she moves into the first of the Bishop poems.

"Where did you find them?" Pere says, when she's finished. "Heard 'em before, never forgot."

All this time wanting to talk to him, waiting to talk with him, and now she's embarrassed.

"First few words and I was ready to . . . if I had my strength, you wouldn't have continued."

"Tell me what happened." Since she's brought it up, she may as well carry through, even though she sees it upsets him.

"Some things are better left untold."

"I'm trying to understand."

"I did what I thought had to be done."

"Did Grandmother know?"

The true fragility of his body stands out as he struggles for words. His eyes water. His cheekbones lift like stones from the smooth surface of his face. The words emerge slowly, delicately, like bubbles of soap.

"When you ran off to Jose's, Claire told me she had known parts of the story for years: gossip. She asked for the whole picture, like you. To her I confessed. It was then she determined to back you up."

"You were so hard on me."

"If the young had the wisdom of the old, life would be different."

Damaris sits erect in her chair, determined to draw more out of him, not to let him escape with evasion. She wants answers. "But why . . . ?" she begins.

"Forgive . . ." he whispers.

"Pardon?"

"Forgive me."

So many words enter her head at once she can't respond, can't filter through her confusion. *Forgive.* With a simple word he asks her to release him from years of rejection and conflict.

Forgive. This word has been spoken before between them, she remembers vaguely. What had happened? Ah, yes. Eight months pregnant, she had gone to Pere to ask forgiveness. Unable to recall their words, she remembers only the tension, the great, sad longing with which she departed; the disappointment.

Before she can speak, Grand-pere closes his eyes and moves

into the sudden sleep that overcomes him more often now. She watches him for a long time. Every now and then, his hand rises into the air, waves back and forth in his sleep. Every now and then, she whispers to unhearing ears, "Why were you so hard?"

August arrives and with it a humid, intense heat. Pere requests a fan, sweats so she must change his sheets twice a day. His brief periods of strength decline. Most of his days are spent sleeping, most of his nights restlessly awake.

"What happens to us when we die?" he asks one night.

"It's not something I've worked out," Damaris says, as calmly as possible, considering the fear that rises in her chest. *Won't be long now.*

"As our bones turn to soil, does our soul survive?"

"Do you want me to call in the minister?"

But he wants no one, wants to be left in peace. Ashes to ashes, dust to dust. These are not questions she can answer, and the struggle to do so leaves her frustrated by all she does not know, by all she cannot say.

"Time to call Peter home," he says one sweltering afternoon, several weeks later.

For a moment that seems like an hour, she does not reply.

"How do you figure that?"

He sighs. "You get wisdom on your deathbed," he says, with closed eyes.

But when Damaris telephones Windhaven to leave a message for Logan to call her, Mrs. Twine reminds her that Logan and Peter have gone.

"Where?"

"Didn't leave an address. Said you'd know how to reach him."

Somewhere on the back burner of her memory, she hears Logan's voice saying "Now write this down, this is where we'll be." Frantically, she searches through the clipboard of scrap paper kept near the phone for messages. She must have written it down. She'd have been a fool not to.

"Calm down, now." Myra Bea on the telephone. "It'll turn up."

But it is still missing several nights later when, as Damaris sits beside Grand-pere's bed, he opens his eyes suddenly and stares. His mouth gapes, he gasps, his leg moves up as if he is about to kick a football, and then down. He is dying. Somehow she knows. The eyes open wider, become cold. Finger on his neck, she feels for a beating vein, but all is still. She remains beside the old man in silence, remains with him for some time, to allow the breath to leave him in peace, to allow herself time to come to believe he is dead.

She takes Grand-pere's hand and rests her cheek in the hollow of the palm, moves her lips against the thumb, feels the rough white hairs on fingers that even now smell of firewood, presses each finger to remember. Remembers his hands on the ropes of the swing, remembers him drawing her back, letting go; she can almost feel him let go now and herself flying forward through the summery air.

15

Humped over the kitchen table in a peony-strewn kimono, Damaris works crossword puzzles from old newspapers and *TV Guides*. In the few days since Pere's death she has lettered many squares. When a puzzle fails to work, she spurns it and begins another.

As soon as Jose hears of Grand-pere's death she arrives, grasping her walker with a determined grip.

"I'm helping until after the funeral—no ifs, ands, or buts." Miraculously revitalized by the challenge of things needing to be done that only Jose knows how to do, to hear her tell, she makes the arrangements with the funeral parlor, organizes the reception.

At first, Damaris protests. After all, it is she who tends to Jose—besides Myra Bea is there to help; but her protestations remain unheard. When ladies from the Episcopal church telephone to sympathize and offer time, Damaris has nothing to keep them occupied. They are her grandparents' friends, after all. Damaris hardly knows them, or so it seems to her. She's more comfortable with Jose and Myra Bea's ministrations.

Myra Bea appears each morning, stays until the evening

light fades. Her intent had been to spend the night, but Damaris has her way.

"No need. I'm fine." But she is not fine. She longs for Peter.

It is Myra Bea who telephones Mrs. Twine, and, learning there is still no sign of Peter, she comforts Damaris.

"After all," Myra Bea says, "it's no great travesty for a child to miss a funeral. His great-grandfather's funeral, no less. When my own grandfather died, the children under thirteen were herded into Grandmother's living room and kept there until the funeral ended."

All the same, Damaris has a need to see the child, to feel the weight of him in her lap, to rest her face against his dry, sun-bleached August hair.

"There are some things we can do nothing about," Myra Bea says. "Though we could alert the police if you knew Logan's license number or the town they're in."

But Damaris does not know, has never found the slip of paper, cannot recall Logan's words.

What's a five-letter word for "bolter"? *Sifts.*
What's a five-letter word for "cafeteria items"? *Trays.*

By the morning of the funeral, she has advanced to puzzles from *The New York Times Magazine*s filched from a neighbor's newspaper stack in his garage.

Overcoming her morning arthritic pain, Jose arrives particularly early to be certain Damaris's house is in order for the reception, but there is not much to be done. That morning, Damaris and Myra Bea scrubbed the kitchen floor. They dusted, vacuumed, put out clean towels, and arranged the silverware and napkins on Grandmother's white-linen tablecloth in the dining room.

What's a seven-letter word for "in general"? *Overall.*
What's a four-letter word for "one of a nautical trio"?
Nina.

Satisfied all is in order, Jose sits across from Damaris, sipping iced tea. "Better finish dressing," she says. "Don't want folks to see you sitting about in disarray."

Damaris nods, doodles on the edge of the puzzle, blackens in a square. As if simply clearing the table, Jose grabs the paper and at last Damaris gets the message.

Hands ink-stained from the leaky pen, she wanders into her bedroom. There awaits the black dress patterned with blue birds, inherited from Miss Winnie. For years regarded as odd for wearing Miss Winnie's hand-me-downs, nowadays she is right in style, though she wears them only on special occasions.

The lightweight wool will be uncomfortable and hot, but it will do. As she reaches behind for the zipper, she remembers the dress she wore the day of her parents' funeral. Grandmother denied that Damaris remembered the funeral, said she'd been too young. But Damaris knows it is memory, mixed in with the repeated story her grandparents told of the event.

That dress, too, had been itchy. Organdy. Purple. The buttons down the back pressed into her skin when she leaned against the spokes of the wooden funeral parlor chair. Time and again the morning of the funeral Grandmother drew the irritating material over her head, and time and again Damaris removed it. Time and again she stamped her patent-leather-shod foot against the floor. She hated the dress. Her foot stung. She wanted to see Mama and Papa. On and off the dress came.

She remembered finally sitting on a stool that played music in a corner of the room by the desk where Grand-pere paid the bills. Remembered his pen, the ink bottle, a stack of envelopes. Grandmother, satisfied she would leave the dress on at last, left the room. The child ruffled the envelopes, attempted to open the ink. The lid stuck. She whacked the bottle on the side of the desk and turned. Ink on her dress, ink on her knees, ink on the pale green Persian carpet. Grandmother's hand on her arm, removing the bottle from her wet grip, shaking her, condemning her to wear the ruined dress to the funeral, black spot and all.

She recalled squirming in the heat, and later, when they lowered the boxes into the ground, she knelt in the grass at the edge. Dirt rolled down the slope, the ink spot stained her dress, Mama, Papa. And then it rained flowers. Daisies and roses, asters and carnations drifted past and quietly covered the brown wood below and their smell in the hot sun made her cry.

By ten-thirty, neighborhood wives begin to arrive with baked goods. The kitchen fills with smells of noodle casseroles, loaves of bread; with the colors of lettuce and Jell-O salads, chocolate and marble layer cakes. They linger, chatting and snacking on pretzels.

When it is time to leave, Damaris pauses in front of the hall mirror, looks into her eyes. If she could turn inside out and enter herself, what would she find? If she could take all the eyes she had ever looked into in the world and line them up on the ceiling, what would she find? What mattered now were Grand-pere's eyes when his breathing stopped. His eyes in the coffin, closed.

Everyone is there: Myra Bea, Jose, Agnes, Josiah and Italo, friends of Pere's Damaris hardly knows. They greet her, commiserate, pay reverence, and later enjoy the feasting.

To Damaris it is a blur. She longs to be in the kitchen in front of a ripping fire even in this heat; has an urge to hide and so hides behind her own facade, which somehow does and says the right things. Stands steady when the coffin is lowered. Sheds tears.

Back home, with hands cold and pale, she greets mourners as they enter the tiny kitchen. Later, when they've gone, she collapses on her bed. Sometime in the afternoon, Myra Bea covers her with a sheet, then later wakes her to share warm leftovers for dinner.

Once more, Myra Bea offers to stay the night.

"I'd rather be alone," Damaris says, and it's true. Kind though Myra Bea is, her boisterous presence is irritating at times. They hug and Damaris realizes with this gesture of friendship that, except for Peter, she has not hugged anyone in a long time.

Long after Myra Bea departs, Damaris rocks in the chair by the stove, staring at unanswered blanks:

What's an eight-letter word for "slender candle"? ——.
What's a six-letter word for "of yore"? ———.

PART · III

16

And now alone these days after Grand-pere's death.

"Coming back to work?" Jose asked the day of the funeral, and Damaris paused. "There's no one like my Damaris," Jose continued. " 'Sides, it'll do you good to keep busy. No sense moping around."

And she means to begin again, she really does, but one morning comes after the other, a week passes, and she hasn't picked up the phone, arranged the schedule.

The house is quiet as she sips her tea, the faint tick-tick-bong of the pendulum clock—their clock—the only sound to break the silence.

Everything in the house belongs to them, little of Damaris's selection, and though she loves it all, a small flicker of longing for something new, her own, arises.

Each day, she traverses the same route, paces from room to room, teacup in hand, planning changes she will make. Pack away Grandmother's dust-gathering knicknacks. Replace the wood-fired monstrosity with a gas stove. New linoleum, a bright color, maybe yellow.

Pere's bedroom smells of stale humanity, trace odors of

uric acid, and the lingering, hard-to-pin-down odor of human flesh in decline. Stripped to the plastic-covered mattress, the hospital bed awaits removal.

In the closet hang his worn cotton shirts, threadbare wool slacks. To them clings still the odor of his shaving lotion, something lemony.

This room she'll turn into a playroom for Peter. Paint the flowered wallpaper white, install low bookshelves and a child-sized table and chairs.

The house examined, she goes out the door and into the shed. Her backbone aches, her constricted muscles long to stretch and evolve, and this longing extends to an urge to reach her hands to the ceiling, to bend and touch the floor.

After a few deep-knee bends, she turns to her worktable. Tacked to the wall above it is one of Logan's envelopes to Peter, constructed of folded and glued brown paper, decorated with his crazy designs. The muted colors intrigue her as they did when she first looked at his sketchbook that Fourth of July, years ago. Here is the true heart of Logan. The part of him she loves. Close up the design is a wild pattern, but from a distance she makes out an oak tree in the forest with leaves all around; a red-headed woodpecker perched in a tangle of roots. With a pencil, she sketches a simplified version. Does she need his permission to use the idea? She shrugs, for now she is playing, nothing solid, but she's tempted, and the more she contemplates the drawing, the more her fingers ache to bring it out in glass.

Grandmother: the final, living link with the past. As if in unconscious sympathy with Grand-pere's death, Grandmother's condition deteriorates. No longer able to form words, she speaks in throaty sounds, croaks, and grunts.

"Hum, hum, hum, baa, baa, baa," she repeats. Her diet, reminiscent of Peter's as an infant, consists of soft foods:

mashed beans and carrots, puréed beef and chicken. The nurses say she has spent the last few days in bed.

Damaris sits with her, holds her hand. One of Grandmother's roommates talks to someone who isn't there.

"Harold," she says. "Harold, time to take out the trash."

Head swirling from the smell of bleach and ammonia, the nursing home's futile attempt to clothe the septic in antiseptic armor, Damaris rests her cheek against Grandmother's pea-green bedspread. Now, at twenty-two, she is the head of the family. It is frightening, this thought, frightening because of all the past mistakes, so many circumstances incited by her own stubborn will.

Grandmother moans, withdraws her hand. The nurse enters to serve lunch. Damaris stands to depart, but before she leaves she bends over the old woman and embraces the passive, unresponsive form before her.

Creamed tuna and peas on toast. Damaris has not felt much like eating, but this simple meal, one Grandmother served for Sunday-night dinners, appeals to her for lunch. Butter for the roux melts in the saucepan for one, when the telephone rings. Logan, at last.

"Has it been hard for you?" Logan asks, once she explains what happened. Does she detect a coolness in his voice?

"It's not as if I didn't expect he'd die sometime." No, it's her own voice that's cool. It's her own heart that is wrapped in ice. Why has she said such a thing? Expectation does not negate sorrow.

"My father's death was slow, as you recall, so sad, so hard. I know you've been through a lot."

"Nothing I won't survive." Even as she speaks she shivers, trembles as if shaken by some unseen hand, the way Grandpere shook her long ago. *Wake up. He replaced your father—he raised you.*

"I'm sorry to burden you further, on top of your recent sorrow, but I have a proposition. . . ."

Damaris is numb. The proposal is for Peter to live in Maine for a time. Marriage to the shepherdess is imminent and Logan has a long-winded reasoning why the arrangement would benefit everyone, particularly Damaris.

". . . a break for you, give you a chance to get back on your feet and . . ."

The words hit her conscious mind, then sink into meaninglessness. This is mad; a crazy idea. Her ear aches against the earpiece; her head throbs; she hates the shepherdess, whoever she is.

"I'm not simply pleading for me," Logan says. "The boy loves it here. I haven't presented the idea to him yet, of course. I'll wait for your decision."

Unable to straighten her thoughts, she finally chokes out, "I don't know . . . I—"

"Please think it over," he says, interrupting her. "I know it's a shock coming out of the blue. Give the idea time to sink in. We'll talk again—say, in two days. I'll call around three o'clock."

After she hangs up, Damaris jabs the can opener into the top of the can of peas and turns, but cannot cut the last section of metal. The lid sinks into the liquid when she tries to lift it with her fingers. By the time she raises it with a knife and dumps the peas into the saucepan on top of the incomplete roux, she has lost the desire to eat.

Upset, she stomps into the backyard. That Logan. Round and round the yard she walks, then into the shed. Work, the solace for all wounds and confusion. On the table, "Ancient Eyes," the old man's face, is leaded up, ready to tack with solder. In these last months her one-window-a-week pace first slowed, then halted. The face has been unfinished for a while. She plugs in the soldering iron and, as it heats, cleans the calme lead joints with oleic acid so the solder will stick. As she begins to solder, her mind is distracted by Logan's proposition and her fingers touch the hot tip of the iron. The pain shocks her, shakes her awake. In seconds, red welts appear on the tips of two fingers and she waves them back and forth in the air as if to cool them.

Back in the house, she tears off an aloe leaf from one of Grandmother's ancient plants and covers her burn with the sticky liquid inside, curses her carelessness, curses Grand-pere for deserting her, curses Logan. She telephones Myra Bea, explains Logan's proposal.

"I'm driving up to talk with him. Want to come?" No need to stand by and wait for his call. She'll take matters into her own hands, put in her two cents in person.

"I can't. I'm deluged with work on this wetlands bill."

"I need company, I—"

"Hold the line a minute."

It comes to Damaris then, as she waits for Myra Bea to return, that she'll steal Logan's sketch, create a window from the ideas he lets lie fallow, become famous with his vision.

"I'm back. Isaac will ride with you. One of my dad's friends. He's headed for Halifax and riding with you partway would save some hitching."

Twenty minutes later, Damaris's bag is packed with toothbrush, toothpaste, comb, and underwear. No time to pack more, no time to think.

Forty minutes later, Damaris fills the tank at the gas station just as Myra Bea's MG sputters in. In the rearview mirror she sees a tall man, as slender as Ichabod Crane, emerge from the car. He wears worn jeans, a T-shirt, a blue denim jacket, and a green cap.

Myra Bea comes to the driver's-side window and introduces him as he climbs in beside Damaris, tosses his satchel into the back.

"I thank you so much. This is wonderful," Isaac says, as he holds out his hand for Damaris to shake.

He has an accent she can't identify; his *wonderful* sounds like *wanderfool,* but his voice is lovely. Flowing and mellifluous; not New England's harsh, choppy dialect. He doesn't look Egyptian.

"Give that Logan what for," Myra Bea says, and she punches Damaris lightly on the arm.

As Damaris eases into the rotary traffic, Isaac squirms in his seat, fidgets with the window. Damaris flicks on the radio, hoping something has changed and it works. Dead as a door nail, whatever that means.

Once they cross the bridge, Isaac relaxes, removes a pack of cigarettes, and pushes in the car lighter.

"These will disturb you?" he asks, indicating the cigarettes.

"No. But I doubt the lighter will work. Not much else does."

Seconds later, the knob pops out, red-hot.

"First time that's been used," she says.

"Absolutely. It is better that way."

"My grandfather never smoked. We're not positive of his exact age, but it's somewhere around ninety. *Was,* I mean. He just died. Probably nothing to do with smoking or not, though."

"I am so sorry to hear that—that he has died, I mean."

"Do you travel a lot?"

"I have been to India, Spain. Got an itch in my butt for new places. Around this beautiful country, too: Colorado, Missouri, Florida."

"My dream is to travel someday."

"You are traveling now, my lady."

The steering wheel is damp from her sweaty hands. On the Southeast Expressway near Quincy they idle in creeping, backlogged traffic. Construction. Her burnt fingers ache and her neck aches, too. Whenever someone passes her in the breakdown lane on the right, she nearly jumps out of her skin.

"There ought to be a law!" she shouts out her window, raising her fist; never mind what Isaac thinks. This is new. Never has she shouted out a car window before.

"Look at this," Isaac says, gesturing toward the convertible beside them. "Shameful, no?"

A pair of teenagers, so close together they look like one fat person, kiss passionately; for them the slow pace means pleasure, not frustration.

Logan and his shepherdess. Did she think he'd remain a bachelor forever, mooning over his lost love, Damaris? Sometimes she wonders where she's been all her life, asleep or in some hazy daydream world. Grand-pere and Logan—the two men in her life—one gone, one soon to be married.

It takes an hour and forty-five minutes to clear the Bunker Hill Monument, normally about a one-hour drive.

"What I would not give for a cup of coffee. You?" Isaac asks, after they have driven for a while.

She thinks about it. "I thought I was tired, but I believe I am hungry. Haven't eaten since breakfast."

"I am famished myself." He reaches into his pocket and removes a ragged map, shakes it open. "I have been this route before. Seem to remember a wonderful diner outside Portsmouth. Let's see. . . ." He runs his finger along the red roads, singing, " 'I am travelin' down this highway heading home. . . .' Here it is. And here are we. Another thirty or forty minutes."

Zeb's Diner is five miles off the highway, a converted railroad car decorated with formica tables and red-plastic-covered stools. Puffy blue plastic lines the walls. They sit at the table farthest from the door.

With the arrival of a waitress, a teenager with a long ponytail and a short skirt, Damaris orders a tuna-salad sandwich with fries and tea. When the waitress turns to Isaac, he checks his wallet.

"For me, just coffee."

"What happened to 'famished'?"

"I had better hang on to the little I have."

"I'll buy you dinner. I mean, you're keeping me company. If you weren't here I'd probably fall asleep at the wheel."

He orders a hamburger, fries, salad, and coffee.

"I love this place," he says. "Pure fifties shit."

She sighs and nods. What does she know? She's only been in the Mummichog Diner, a narrow, plywood box.

"How did you find it?"

"Pure chance. Everything in life is pure chance, no?"

Pure chance. Wasn't there a point in any event when a person could choose? Or at least choose not to choose? What has she chosen for herself with full clarity of vision? Perhaps nothing. Perhaps she's spent most of her life as if she were playing Scrabble—waiting for the perfect letters to turn up, waiting for chance to form the winning combination.

"That's a great cap," she says, when Isaac removes the green hat and sets it on the seat beside him.

"Ah, this. Bought this in Oklahoma, of all places."

She laughs. "No cowboy hat?"

When the waitress arrives with their dinner he says, "You know, out west, everything is bigger, from cockroaches to cocks. That's why I bought this little number. . . ."

Damaris blushes, eyes the waitress. She is certain he wanted the girl to hear, enjoys shaking people up.

He eats lustfully, forks french fries with zest, rams hamburger into his mouth along with salad.

"What were you doing in Oklahoma?"

"I am a musician, down and out at the moment, but all anyone wants me to do is teach Russian."

"Oh. Say something to me."

"Like what?"

"Say 'Good afternoon, Damaris.'" It would be strange to hear her name in Russian.

Instead, he quotes a poem. "Do you recognize?"

"How could I? I don't know Russian."

"Listen to the rhythm." He quotes more lines.

"I like the way it sounds."

"But you do not know?"

"I'm not much good at poetry, although I had a friend once who wrote it."

> The woods are lovely, dark and deep.
> But I have promises to keep,
> And miles to go before I sleep,
> And miles to go before I sleep.

He pauses, waiting for an answer, she supposes, but what she gives him is a frown.

"Robert Frost. 'Stopping by Woods on a Snowy Evening.'"

"Oh. I ought to know it."

He shrugs.

"How do you come to know Russian?"

"That *I* ought to know. I was born there."

That's why his speech sounds slightly strange, melodic, with a few odd pronunciations. She feels ignorant, foolish.

"I wish I understood another language. I never finished high school."

"That I would never have guessed," he mumbles.

She finishes her sandwich and nods at her fries.

"Hmm?" she questions, the sound deep in her throat.

"Uh-huh," he replies, and she scrapes her fries onto his plate, as if they have been doing this for years.

On impulse, outside of Portsmouth, she hits Route 1. Longer, but more scenic. Less traffic.

"Look at this landscape," Isaac says. "For six months I

lived with a friend in the mountains. Lived in a log cabin in the middle of the woods. For hours you drove on a dirt road in the Jeep, then for miles on nothing but a cow path.

"Six months and all I did was play my cello and gaze out the window. One cloudy afternoon I watched the trees for hours. So much moisture in the air the trees peeked through the fog as if covered in gauze. I returned to my music, and later when I looked up, the treetops had disappeared. Completely. Several hours later, I panicked. Thought I saw fires everywhere as wisps of moisture floated up like smoke," he says, demonstrating the path of the dispersing fog with his hands.

They drive for another forty minutes or so when the car lurches and the dashboard lights up. She stops on the shoulder and they both get out. He checks the tires, she opens the hood. Oil covers the inside of the hood, the engine, and oil case.

"The dipstick measures 'fill,' " she says.

"Wonderful. An empty highway and no gas station in sight."

He stands near her, slightly to the side and behind. Their fingers touch as he takes the dipstick and checks the oil level for himself.

" 'I am travelin' down this highway headin' home, and once there no more I'll roam. . . .' " he sings through his teeth. "You are absolutely right. No oil."

"Now that you've confirmed it, it's true."

"Of course. That is the way of the world—it is the man's opinion that counts."

As she slams down the hood, her sleeve brushes his arm, she smells his tobacco.

"Do they have call boxes on this flea-bitten highway?"

"Call boxes," she repeats like a fool.

"Maybe a cop will come along."

They sit on the hill beside the car.

"Can I have a cigarette?" she asks. She lights up and they smoke in silence. A car passes, slows, but doesn't stop. It strikes her as funny that she's asked for a cigarette. Hasn't smoked since she was seventeen.

"Idyllic," he says.

Oh, yes, idyllic to be stuck on this road in a junk-heap car not much longer for this world. *Won't be long now.* Grandpere's voice comes to her and then the image of him lying on the hospital bed and suddenly she is weak and light, as if she's left some part of her thinking mechanism behind, and maybe her blood and bones, too, and she's a fragile, hollow form sitting with a stranger.

"Might be a station down the road," she says, rising and stomping out the cigarette in the sand. "Want to walk?"

He shakes his head, lies back in the grass, and closes his eyes.

Heading north, she turns away from him. This will delay her far too long. She wants her arms around Peter, now. She kicks the pebbles beside the road. She likes Isaac. Likes the way he is easy, lolls on the grass, not worried, but then, why would he be? He can always hitch a ride. She hopes he doesn't. Funny the way he sings now and then. Except for Grandmother's "Froggie" renditions, she hasn't heard singing for ages, has listened only to some faint humming in her ears, but no music.

After awhile of seeing nothing, not even a house, she returns. The flashing lights of a police car light up the highway. The passing driver must have reported them.

"Called a tow truck," the cop says. "Be here in half an hour."

They ride in the tow truck to Patsy's Garage in town. Patsy, a burly man with a long, thin moustache, says, "Be early tomorrow before I can even look at it."

"I'm in a hurry," she says.

"I'll do my best, but it's already after six."

They remove their bags and leave the garage. Main Street consists of two blocks of dingy stores selling pizza and newspapers. The hardware store specializes in cobwebs and dust; the post office is hidden in the rear of a curio shop.

"I don't believe it," Damaris says. "Do you see a motel?"

"Relax. It is okay. We will look in a phone book."

In the drugstore, they find a telephone. The one motel listed is three miles out of town. Walkable. Before leaving the store, Damaris buys a crossword-puzzle magazine.

"I guess you'll want to take your bag up to the highway and hitch another ride."

"Or, on the other hand, I could at least escort you to the motel. Ensure you arrive safely."

His company pleases her. After a few blocks, the sidewalk ends and they find themselves on the shoulder. As they walk, she notices his shoes for the first time. Somehow they look foreign: worn, thin, black-leather tie shoes. Shoes like no one she knows would wear. Suddenly, he weaves and bumps into her as if he is drunk.

"You okay?"

"Sorry," he says. "I keep thinking about the friends I am about to visit. Maybe I should not go. I do not know what to do."

"Ah. A man who can't make decisions."

"Absolutely. One of my major flaws and one reason I do not mind the delay."

"What do you mean?"

"Of course, I should not talk about it to a total . . . well, almost total stranger." They walk in silence for a time. "But after all, you are a friend of Myra's." Farther down the road, he continues: "He is my best friend, you see, and whenever I visit, his wife tries to . . . well . . . you know."

"And you don't like that." She doesn't know what he's

talking about, but figures if she waits it will become clear.

"It is not a matter of liking or not. It is a matter of . . . propriety. For one thing, she is only sixteen. A child. I am thirty. Of course, he is my age, but I feel old enough as it is without screwing around with a woman who could almost be my daughter, my best friend's wife."

"Such problems." Sounds like a television show; melodramatic. But he seems seriously concerned.

"The permutations of love. Thing is, this time he will be gone for a few days. She will be there alone. This sort of thing has never happened to you?"

She shakes her head, almost tells him about Logan and herself, but it wasn't the same. They walk in silence for a while. Suddenly, she feels as if her life has been narrow, constricted. The permutations of love. If Logan can find a new love, so can she, and that small flicker of longing for something new that flared soon after Grand-pere died flares once more.

"Hold this," she says, handing him her bag. She walks fast, then runs.

"Slow down!" he shouts. "We might as well enjoy the evening, no?"

When she reaches a boulder, she sits and waits. He might think she doesn't like him if she runs too far. Might change his mind and leave.

The pink-stucco motel sits back from the road. She takes a single room, offers to share with him. The room is dingy, small; the windows overlook a dried-up stream and field of broken-down cars.

Isaac flips the television stations. "We have an old Grace Kelly movie, Lucille Ball. I do not know . . . what do you like?"

"I don't care." She flops on the bed, exhausted.

"Ah. A woman who cannot make decisions."

"We have so much in common," she says, as she rolls onto her side and rests her head on her arm to watch him.

"So we will see what I want." He flips to the news, pushes two chairs together, sits on one and props his feet on the other.

"What was it like, growing up there?" she asks tentatively, curious, but not wanting to pry.

"Of course, everybody wants to know about Russia. . . ."

"You hear so many things and sometimes don't know what's real and what's not."

"*You* meet new people and what do you talk about? Your job, what movies you like. *I* meet people and they only want to talk about Russia."

"I guess I'm pretty naïve. In some ways, I feel everyone in the world is like me. I mean, we all sleep and get up and eat. We all think and want to hold loved ones. Things like that. And the difference is, in some places it's easier to do those things than in others."

He looks at her, rubs his hand against his high, thin forehead. "Well, I do not know what you are saying, really."

He switches television stations and they watch a movie.

"It's almost as if we're friends," she says. He reaches over and squeezes her knee. At ten, she climbs into bed, wearing her jeans and T-shirt. She tosses a pillow at him; he laughs and throws it back. She clutches it to her chest and when he comes to retrieve it he bends over, kisses her forehead.

"Good night." He returns to his chairs, turns off the lights, turns down the sound on the television.

Covers up to her chin, she burrows down, relishes the weight of the sheet and the way her body can be cool when she first enters bed and then warmth builds up, creating a cave of heat and her own perfume. Through half-closed eyes she peers at Isaac. The television light flickers patterns on his face.

The first time he removed his cap in the diner, her heart

went out to him. Short hair, scalp showing through. The shape of his head makes her want to take her hand and run it over the flatness at the back of his skull, to pull his head against her breast. She envisions him as a child: large head, thin neck, inquisitive expression questioning the reason for doing something, while at the same time resigned to doing it. She's seen that expression on Peter's face enough times to sense it there in Isaac's. She tosses and turns until, after a long time, her eyes close.

"Be ready by five this afternoon," Patsy says, on the telephone the next morning. "It was the module, plus an oil leak."

"It *can* be fixed, can't it?"

"Ordered a new part. Should get 'er by noon. But you'll have to keep an eye on that oil from now on."

Isaac sleeps under a twisted blanket in his chairs. His rumpled shirt has a hole in it and one sock is inside out. He opens his eyes and looks at her.

"We're stuck until five."

He shrugs, adjusts his position, and rests his feet on the floor. "I hate mornings," he says, rubbing his face.

Here they differ. Mornings are her best time. When she returns from the motel coffee shop with coffee, tea, and sticky buns on a large plastic tray, he is still in the same position.

"I think I got it right. Cream?"

She sets his cup on the table and flicks on the "Today" show. "Norman Mailer's being interviewed."

"Oh," he says. He lifts his head and stares at the picture for a moment. "Turn that off, will you, please?"

She sits on the bed with her tea. Last night she slept restlessly, imagining an encounter between Isaac and herself, imagining waking beside him, kissing him.

"My skin feels swollen, hot." She touches her face. "Maybe a fever from worrying about the car."

"Relax. Take things as they come."

"Feel my head. What do you think?"

He touches her forehead. "Maybe you should spend the day under the covers. A day like that never hurt anyone."

"Maybe."

"I am still thinking about my problem."

"Relax," she says. "Take things as they come."

They laugh. He stands and stretches. "Well, I will not hold you again in the thrall of my woes."

A great desire to talk rises up in her like a fever; she almost tells him of her woes. He seems to understand the facets of sorrow, but what would he know of being a parent?

"I guess I will shower," he says.

As he removes his shirt, Damaris opens the crossword-puzzle magazine she bought in town.

"Hold it. What is this? You like puzzles?"

"What's a six-letter word for 'insurrection'?"

"Wait a minute, wait a minute," he says, putting his shirt on again. "I have an idea. We will race. I will do the puzzle on the page opposite yours."

"I know who'll win. I'm slow as a turtle."

"Where is another pencil?"

They sit side by side on the bed, using the tray as a desk.

After twenty minutes of silence, punctuated only by Isaac's curses and moans as he struggles with the clues, he shouts, "Winner! Now I will help the poor high-school dropout with hers."

Damaris has the childish urge to stick her tongue out at him, but instead she playfully whacks his arm, his arm that then leans warmly against hers as they finish her puzzle.

They race several more times until Damaris, tired of losing, awards Isaac the honorary title of Crossword Champion.

"And you are first runner-up," he says.

Damaris flips the booklet shut and is about to throw it at him when he grabs her wrist to halt her, and in this moment she wants him to hold her, to take her up and out of her isolate self into worldly communion. He releases her wrist, moves away slowly, as if pondering a great question. The moment for closeness is lost, hesitation at fault.

Slowly he rises from the bed, states once more his intent to shower. "How about you? You want to go first?"

She declines and lies on the bed, listening to the shower. The water beats a swift rhythm against the tile walls, matches the beat of her heart.

Five minutes later he calls her name. Steam pours out of the bathroom as he stands in the open doorway like a tree in the fog. A branch, his arm, waves in the air as he signals her.

"What is it?" she asks. "Is something wrong?"

When she reaches his side, he kisses her. A brief kiss, but she leans toward him to return it. He is wet and her clothes become wet, too, when he draws her to him, leads her into the bathroom, eases off her shirt. As he unbuckles her belt, unzips her jeans, he kisses her. She kicks off her sandals, pushes her jeans to the floor. He draws the shower curtain aside and they step into the steam.

Water hits her skin, soaks her hair in seconds. He presses his hands against the back of her neck, then down her spine, touching each vertebra until he reaches the last bone and moves her toward him.

The Blue Crab River, she is in the river and something sweeps her deep, deep out into the bay and deeper where electric fishes live, where it's dark, no air, no soil to rest her feet on, nothing to hold onto as she descends farther, farther. There are only Isaac and Damaris in the shower.

Then later, out of the shower and onto the bed.

"How do you feel?" he asks, as he pushes the covers to one side.

Except for a few moments in her life—giving birth, with Logan—she hasn't thought about her body unless a pain came, a twinge, a hunger.

"Are you comfortable?"

"Yes."

"Tell me how you feel."

"Good," she says, as blood rushes to muscles that had been numb.

"Say it in my ear. Say my name."

"Isaac, I feel good." Her lips brush his earlobe, she reaches for the wall above her, and he grasps her wrists, holds them over her head.

"My name."

"Isaac."

"Do you feel good?" His knees press her thighs.

"Yes."

"My name." Deep, deeper.

"Isaac."

"My name."

"Isaac."

"Isaac."

I-S-A-A-C.

By five-fifteen, they are on the highway once more.

"One-hundred and sixty dollars," she says. "And for what? The car'll be ready for the junkyard any minute."

According to the map, Route 1 heads directly into Fairweather Harbor, then continues up the coast. The closer they get, the more anxious she becomes. As she drives, she whispers to herself, bites her lip.

"I think you are distressed," Isaac says. "I see this in your face."

She grips the wheel firmly. Her hands sweat once again, as they had on the Southeast Expressway.

"What is it? Missing the ferry? Are you worried about that?"

"In part, I guess. . . ." She glances at him. His face is interested, kindly. "It's my son. His father is getting married and wants Peter to live with him, and I . . . but not being a parent, this might be hard for you to understand."

"Try me."

And so she tells her story: her parents' death, meeting Logan, Grand-pere's banishment, the first grim island visit.

"On the one hand, never having had a father myself, I know it's important for Peter to be with Logan. I don't want to deprive him of that chance. On the other . . . well, I'm his mother . . ."

"And you will be his mother all your life. That does not end."

"No. I suppose not."

"I will tell you now of me. I left behind two children. Daughters. I have been in this country five years. . . . They are eight and ten now."

"How sad."

"Sad. But necessary sometimes. In this case, the girls are better off with their mother."

"Do you ever see them?"

"Now and then the restrictions on visitors are lifted. Then I go. When the atmosphere is right. So, you see, I know a little how you must feel."

He touches her cheek, looks at her with his serious gaze. Somehow her problem shrinks beside his, seems small, almost petty, a minor issue in the world of sorrows about her. How selfishly blind she has been, as if wandering in a dark wood, gazing inward and only now emerging into the bright light, only now gazing about her to see others' sorrow, to see things right in front of her eyes that she hadn't seen before.

"Of course, with a boy, perhaps it is a father's hand he needs."

"My purse," she says, waving a hand toward the seat. "Handkerchief, please."

He removes a square of pink linen from her purse. "One of these, I have not seen in a long time."

Here they are, she thinks, as she wipes her tears. Born on opposite sides of the globe and struggling with such similar sorrows and separations. This is what she'd been trying to tell him in the motel room when she'd said, "I guess I feel everyone in the world is like me." But she'd said it so awkwardly, he hadn't understood. Her words rarely seem to describe things the way she feels them inside.

"You will be okay? Should I drive?" he asks softly.

"Check out that sign up ahead."

"Let me see. It says FAIRWEATHER HARBOR—TEN MILES."

"I can make it for ten miles."

At the ferry landing, they exchange addresses, promise to keep in touch.

"I wish you luck with your dilemma," he says.

"And you with yours."

"Hang loose," he says, as he tips his cap and crosses the road to thumb a ride.

The last ferry had departed sometime earlier, at four-thirty; Damaris must spend the night in her car. A soft moon spreads a faint light over the old blue wagon as she opens the tail gate and lowers the seat. Spreading towels against the metal bed, she lies on her back, covers herself with a worn beach blanket.

The maple leaves move back and forth with the breeze; the night sky is clear. Restless and awake, she tosses and turns, wonders what it would be like if the station wagon began to move on its own along the black-tar road, flowing with the curves of bright yellow down the center. Maybe the old blue wagon would take her clear up to the top of the world, as far as a person could go. Maybe beyond, right up to the stars, right up into the heart of those ancient eyes that glitter their greeting each night.

17

Logan has shingled the cabin, painted the window trim gray. In the front room, a bentwood couch replaces the bed. Chairs, a bookcase, and a rose-toned carpet create a decent parlor. The painted room is now the dining area, and a large bedstead and small cot fill the room where old man Perth once slept. No one around, no sign of the shepherdess.

The morning ferry arrived on Windhaven at ten A.M. and Damaris dragged Jeremiah away from the inn to transport her once again to Logan's. He will return for her before dark.

Behind the cabin, in the weedy garden, tufts of carrots, beets, and turnips appear. She picks a carrot, washes it at the sink. Here is a change; a sink with faucets. And another; an indoor bathroom. She slices the carrot and sits on the front stoop eating. Flower beds line the slate walk: nasturtiums, marigolds, and a thin rosebush with three yellow flowers. Old Skate rests in a cushion of sand and stares at her with mournful eyes. Where are they?

A trail cuts through the pine grove and Damaris walks for a time. The ground moss is soft and smooth under her feet; the leaves flicker with platinum light. The sound of axe against wood rises from deep in the grove. Human voices mingle with a dog's bark as she reaches a small clearing.

Through the branches shines the red of Peter's shirt. Beside him, Logan raises the axe, then a swift downward movement as he lowers axe into wood. Peter fills a wheelbarrow, taking over her job as assistant. They work well together, father and son. Beyond them graze a white, fluffy herd. Sheep.

She moves into the clearing. No one speaks for a moment; then Logan walks toward her, holds out his arms to embrace her.

She steps aside, out of reach.

Logan shrugs amiably. "What a surprise."

Peter runs to her, clasps her around the waist in a bear hug. She stoops.

"Missed you," she says, hugging him back. "Love you."

A dog barks; a yellow puppy emerges from behind the woodpile, joins them eagerly.

Peter releases her, kneels, embraces the squirming dog.

When she stands, the sun is bright in her eyes and she blinks. The two, boy and pup, blend into a bronze stroke of light, as if on fire.

"The sheep have arrived. Where is the shepherdess?" Hard as she tries to remain neutral, a bitterness creeps into her voice.

"Marla will come in October."

"The wedding?" Damaris had, after all, had her chance to be part of the island life. She rejected it then; she'd reject it now, if offered.

"Damaris . . . I've known Marla all my life. We were close long before she moved to Canada . . . we once thought of marrying years ago—"

"Now, about your suggestion," Damaris interrupts, as calmly as possible, quieting her beating heart with simple words. Once she intended to scream, to yell if necessary, but talking with Isaac calmed her. Logan's eternal calmness calms her.

Logan takes her arm lightly. "Let's go back to the house. We'll talk."

They move down the path. Peter and the dog traipse behind.

Damaris stumbles on a mound of dirt and Logan tightens his grip. He wants Peter with him. "Peter," Damaris says, and turns to look at the boy. In the cradle, she'd cared for him in the cradle, then scraping his knees on the pavement, falling from his tricycle. She shakes her arm away from Logan and waits for the child, walks beside him, holds his hand.

In the dining room, the pup lies panting under the table; Peter runs his sneaker down its back. Damaris is dizzy, her head hot. Why has she never given him a dog?

"Peter loves it here," Logan says. "Don't you, son?" He ruffles Peter's hair and the boy ducks his head. "He needs a father."

With a boy perhaps it is a father's hand he needs, Isaac said, and she knows he does, can see he does.

Don't let him go, something deep inside her whispers, so softly she barely hears.

"You have no legal right, you know." Her eyes burn, feel puffy. The sun has made her tired, confused.

"You're upset. You've been through a lot."

Unfair. It is all unfair. Grand-pere . . . Peter . . . Her chest itches as if she has a rash. She adds tea to her glass from the heavy crystal pitcher; the copper-colored liquid spills on her hand, on the table.

"I'll wipe it up," Peter says. He returns with a flannel rag to absorb the spill. She places her hand on his and they move together, round and round in a circle. The rag swells with tea. A great wave of sorrow rises within her, as if absorbed from the universe. Hot. The underside of her tongue, her ears, and forehead. Run-down. No sleep. Lack of sleep always makes her ill.

"He would hate it here in the winter."

"Are you talking about *me?*" Peter asks.

Logan nods at the boy in answer to his question. "How do you know what he'd like till he tries it."

How does a person know anything? How does a person know anything for sure except that the earth is round and spins through the universe, that the sun rises and brings warmth, that the mysterious moon waxes and wanes.

"He almost died that winter."

Peter plays peek-a-boo from behind Logan. His silver hair and pale forehead loom above his father's darkness. The boy is lucky to have Logan, lucky to have someone beside herself. *A man's touch.* But the shepherdess . . .

Logan reaches across the table, places his hand on her forearm. "This isn't easy," he says.

Aches. She aches from her buttocks down the back of her legs. *Stand up for what you want.* The whisper again. Weak, head heavy, she rises, wanders to the front door, balances on the threshold. She had no doorstep to turn up on but Pere's. *Don't let him go. Too young.*

"Are you all right? You look pale," Logan says, coming up beside her.

Does she project some mistaken idea of fragility? Of course she's all right. Now, in the midst of wanting to lie on the floor, she knows she is all right, knows she's been all right all along.

"Dizzy. The heat."

"Come sit in the lawn chair. There's a cooling breeze off the bay."

He leads her to a sagging blue-and-white-striped chair and she feels infinitely lonely. Things go on and on for years in the same way and then what happens? Is it in the conjunction of the stars for change to occur? Pure chance? Simply the way of the world?

Logan's hands are cool on her neck, on her shoulders as he eases her down. A cool palm on her forehead.

"You are hot."

The confirmation. Like Isaac. *No oil.*

"Let's not talk anymore today. Let's let it rest until tomorrow," Logan says.

"I'm leaving tonight."

Leaving. *Isaac closed the car door, reached in to her behind the wheel, his face soft and kind. "Hang loose," and she watched him cross the road to thumb a ride north.* He will call her the next time he's at the Rossiters's.

Logan speaks, but her ears are full of water rushing and wind in the trees and she cannot hear. She wants to kneel on the ground, cool her face on the walkway slates.

Logan takes her hands, lifts her from the chair. "You'd best go to bed."

"Bed?"

Bed. Light plays off the wall of painted leaves as he leads her through the dining room into the bedroom, helps her into bed, covers her with the sheet.

Isaac. Isaac had pulled her across the mattress, had held her arms over her head. She shivers. "Leaving," she says, and Logan whispers something, his tone reassuring.

The back of her neck is hot, the nodes swollen. Someone wraps a light cover around her, heat surrounds her, she sinks deeper and deeper into the dark.

Later, she wakes, moans. Someone applies a wet cloth to her eyes, lips. Voices. Movement. A door slams. *Isaac slammed the door and crossed the road. Pure chance.* Someone sits beside her, caresses her forehead. With great effort she opens her eyes. Logan.

"I have to go home . . ." she says, trying to sit. Skate, lying at the foot of the bed, thumps his tail on the floor.

"My car . . ." She must find her car, leave this place, Grand-pere needs her. No. For a moment she forgot. He lies in the North Osprey Cemetery; his final date awaits carving.

Water. Logan with the cloth against her neck. This is what it must feel like to be old. What Grand-pere felt when he lay helpless, unable to rise and do what needed to be done. And it is now that the sadness hits her in full, the great sorrow of Grand-pere's loss. Grand-pere. Now she understands . . . well, maybe not understands, but feels somehow what he feared all those years: the leavings, the betrayals, the lone-liness, the confusion.

As a child she'd seen him as an ugly ogre, but the child vision dissolves now and Grand-pere seems a mere man, sim-ply human. All she ever wanted was to be close to him, and when at last he asked her forgiveness, she had not given it.

She slackens into blackness again. Lies in bed, hour after hour. Days pass: one, two, three. She clocks them by the sun; beaming on her at times, then not, then on. Chaotic thoughts swirl around and around, in and out: now Peter needs his lunch, now he's an infant once more, diapers to wash, bottles to fill. Now before her in disarray whirl the contents of Jose's closets: old, musty pillows, high-heeled rubber boots, sheaves of blurred, typewritten pages, years' worth of accumulated goods once necessary, now abandoned. Abandoned.

Someone stands over her with a cup of spring water. She swallows; her tongue is dry in spite of the fluids. "Rest," a voice says, and someone dips the cloth, wrings it out, bathes her with care.

Once more she sleeps the nightmare, hallucinatory sleep. Wakes again to the dark. Fluids taken clamor for release. She places her feet on the floor, staggers, reaches for the bedpost. Logan's nightshirt. How did she get into his nightshirt? And why is she in old man Perth's bed? Confused, she's in another time, years earlier. Where is the old man? Where is the baby?

She crosses slowly to the door, then past the painted walls, past Logan and a young boy asleep on the floor; out into the night she wanders in search of the outhouse. Here is the tool shed, *here is the church,* here is the chicken coop, *here is the steeple.* But the outhouse: demolished. Crazy Logan tore it down. What to do, what to do?

Crouch, of course. On the path through the woods she finds a hidden spot behind a large pine tree. Like camping. Like Girl Scouts. Be prepared.

The woods are cool. Quiet. She wanders farther along the path, the ground beneath her feet is warm, living, almost human. She tramples earth's flesh, earth's backbone. Simply living earth, simply human.

Someone takes her hand, some invisible someone leads her to the far end of the island, where she climbs the Ice Age boulder, gazes out over the sea. The rock, alive, too, with silvery mica, warm under her feet from the daytime sun, is lined as an ancient face, lined as Grand-pere's, Miss Winnie's, Grandmother's, the Wampanoag woman from the fair long ago.

"Love is the medium through which your wisdom will come." Love. The water rolls and hisses about the rock, dampens her foot like a kiss.

The smell of salt and kelp clears her head, the fever crests, and she knows for sure she must not let him go, the boy, not yet. *Too young.* In one brief flash of vision her world aligns, and magically, as if the lid of a music box has been lifted by a silent hand, music plays in her. A hum from deep within. She touches her chest and feels the sound, large, larger. She moves her fingers to her throat, one hand on either side of her larynx, presses until she feels her pulse, as she had felt for Grand-pere's the night his heart let go of the beating. But her heart beats on, she feels it in her fingers, hears its echo in the rhythm of the hissing waves at her feet. And then she comes down into a smooth clearness, but tired, so tired.

She returns to the path through the woods. *"And miles to go before I sleep . . .* She must rest. Here. A bed of leaves. Rest.

A hand presses into her shoulder. Once more in bed, she opens her eyes to light and whiteness. The hand is no hand, but a paw. Skate. She smells clean smells: soap, the sun beaming through the window. A fly hangs in a cobweb in the corner, jiggling up and down, trying to escape.

Logan appears. "So you're back with us. Thought we'd lost you last night. I found the bed empty and you asleep on the path. Remember?"

He props pillows behind her back, returns with chicken broth. It feels good on her throat. The tight clutch of illness dissolves. "You've been kind. I thank you," she says, and then she tells Logan of her decision. ". . . too young. Maybe when he's older, when he can be part of the decision," she says, though she doesn't know if she'd ever agree to part from Peter.

"It was a long shot," Logan says, "but I thought I'd try."

That evening she eats poached eggs on toast; they remind her of Miss Winnie. She has no more fever.

Several days later, she sits outside. The shade of the maple protects her from the late-afternoon sun. Behind the cabin, Logan and Peter stack wood for the winter on the ever-present, undulating line. The pup yips and yowls about their feet. Like a golden streak of fire, the dog races to retrieve a twig Logan tosses in the air. Then down the length of the woodpile and up the other side runs the creature with Peter in pursuit. Round and round until boy catches dog and they fall to the ground, wrestling for the twig. And then they are up and running, racing toward her, singing a breathless tune of barks and boyish shouts.

"Are you better now?" Peter asks, his face solemn. His arm drapes lightly around her neck.

"Much better."

"I'm sad about Pa."

"So am I."

"I made him a present."

"Did you?"

"Dad says I'll never see Pa again."

"Never again."

"But I'll see Dad again, won't I?"

"You'll visit next summer, no doubt," she says, though she knows there are no guarantees. Her parents. Grand-pere.

Logan approaches, draws up a lawn chair. "You're certain you'll take him?"

She nods.

"I am disappointed, needless to say. But you are right. I have no legal claim, no claim but blood. I'm sorry things didn't work out between us," he says, taking her hand. "I've never known. Was it something I did? Failed to do?"

"I . . ." Damaris says, stammering, about to remind him of the time when death grinned, but she stops. Before her eyes Logan changes. No, it is not Logan who changes; her vision shifts. Shifts as it had the first time she'd seen Logan's painted wall. The wall seemed a maze of colors and indefinite shapes at first, but then her vision had adjusted and she saw what had been there all along, the finer details of a world full of animals and plants.

Peter's illness was no more Logan's fault than her own.

"It had nothing to do with you, only myself." *Only my own closed heart, closed mind.*

"What happened here?" he asks, as he runs his finger over the scars from her burns.

"Carelessness." Not looking. Not paying attention. The scars in her life seem to come from not looking, not seeing things as they are. When she first burned herself she thought she was angry about Logan's marriage, but no—not anger—just the pain flowing—just the sorrow releasing its clasp.

Somehow his marriage sets her straight in her thinking. It was not love they had together, Damaris and Logan. Not from him to her—had he ever *said* he loved her?—not from her to him. His art drew her to him; his tapestry paintings. An illusion—love.

"Friends?" Logan asks, and he tugs her hand as if already shaking in agreement. But he has the wrong hand, she thinks, he has the left when it should be the right.

"Friends."

And so they return, Damaris and Peter. The ferry hums. Gulls ride on the wind behind the boat, screeching as they dive for chunks of bread and crackers thrown to them by tourists. Today the vessel is crowded with anxious parents, whiny children, elderly couples exclaiming over the beauty of the world.

From the deck, Damaris and Peter wave to Logan until he recedes into a small, brown speck on the dock. As the dock fades out of sight, Peter grasps the boat rail with one hand and with the other clings to Damaris's fingers. They ache slightly, her fingers; she longs to grip the glass cutter once more, to piece together her version of Logan's designs.

Packed in a carton are some of his sketches she'll translate into windows. No stealing necessary. If she succeeds, he will send more. They'll work out a deal, businesswise.

Hypnotically, the water churns and froths below. The sun is bright on the water, Damaris must half-shut her eyes against the glare, almost copper. Peter stares, too, leans slightly forward, as if he might float on the crest of the waves.

"Look," he says, pointing out over the water. "Is it a whale?"

Out in the bay, a large fish leaps and brings to mind the whales beached off Wellfleet not long ago. They died, the lot of them, fifteen or twenty there had been, severed from the sea, stranded to die, some sort of natural sacrifice.

"I believe it's only a large fish," Damaris says.

"Will you go with me to the other side?" Peter asks, looking up at Damaris.

"Other side?" Suddenly she thinks of Pere. Of Twyla and Mitchell. Of Grandmother, soon. Crossing to the other side. How does Peter know this phrase?

"You know. The front. The part that's pointed where we're going."

"Oh. The prow."

"Yes. Will you walk me to the brow? I'm brave, you know. I'm not afraid I'll fall off."

"Of course not. Though I admit to being somewhat afraid myself."

Peter laughs. "Grown-ups don't get afraid."

"Well, they certainly need a hand to hold now and then," Damaris says, and the two begin a slow-paced walk around the deck, weaving their way among the mass of tourists.

EPILOGUE

One afternoon, several days after their return to North Osprey, Damaris looks up from her work to find Peter standing
in the doorway to the shed, holding the gift he and Logan
had made on the island for Grand-pere.

"It was lost in my suitcase."

She pushes aside the stack of drawings she's been working
on and pats the stool beside her. "Come sit." Above her head,
propped against the window, "Ancient Eyes" catches the
afternoon light.

"We made it 'specially for Pa," Peter says, as he hikes
himself onto the seat.

"Let's see."

Peter unknots the string. "We didn't have ribbon. Dad said
string goes better with brown paper."

"String is perfect."

"The wrapping's a picture. Dad let me use his paints."

Dad this, Dad that. Ever since his return from the island,
the boy chatters nonstop about Logan; follows Damaris
around when she cleans and cooks, reports every detail of
his summer visit, every word Logan said.

Peter removes the tape, his face solemn and serious.

"Is this the same kid who shreds his birthday wrappings?" she asks, trying to lighten the mood, but the child ignores her and unfolds the painting.

"You're sure your dad didn't do this?" she asks, taking the picture, smoothing the folds. With four thumbtacks, she pins the painting to the wall next to Logan's envelope. By the time she's done, Peter removes a small, carved boat from the box.

"You tie a string to this hook and float it in the bay," he says, turning the boat around and around.

"Why don't we try it out?"

"Dad says sailing boats is man-to-man stuff."

"Women play with boats, too, kiddo."

"Too short," he says, holding up the scraps of string.

"There's a longer piece here somewhere," she says, searching through the drawers until she finds it.

With the boat in hand, they set off down the path to the marsh, the same path she and Logan had traversed so many years before. Still one of her favorite haunts, she has not been there this summer.

The afternoon heat smothers sounds. The birds are quiet, no hum of human voices to be heard, just the snap and crunch of branches under their feet as they hike together through the woods. The spot has been abandoned in the last few years by all but the November hunters. Overgrown from disuse, the path is almost as hidden and mysterious as it had been thirty years before.

They follow the rough terrain up the hill and down the other side. At the bottom of the hill they emerge from the dark overgrown coolness of the woods into the hot, bright flatland of the marsh, cooled by the sea breeze.

The wet and spongy peat hisses beneath their sneakers as the water recedes from the earlier high tide. Sea lavender in its last bloom and tiny white and purple flowers are scattered

through the grass, flowers Damaris means to identify someday. Fiddler crabs scurry and click into hiding as Damaris
and Peter cross the peat to the banks of the Blue Crab River.

The boy kneels in the knee-high grass that lines the muddy,
mussel-strewn banks. He sets the boat into the water and
unwinds the string. Following the current, the boat heads out
toward the bay. For much of the afternoon they take turns
running along the soggy shoreline, steering the boat as best
they can, string in hand as if they are flying a kite.

The sun moves closer to the gleaming knob atop the railroad bridge, the riverbanks enlarge as the waterline recedes.
A gull dives for his dinner.

"One more sail and then home for our dinner," Damaris
says at last, and the boy releases the string as far as it will go.

Damaris crosses the peat to stand on the once-magical spot
where Peter was conceived, where her parents fell in love.
She had been so young and foolish those years before, or so
it now seems. She thought Logan as cold as the wind, as hard
as granite, when all along it was her own heart that was
frozen, her own heart unwilling to yield. "It's the wisdom
holds the power." That's what the Wampanoag woman had
said, and though Damaris is foolish more often than wise
. . . perhaps next time . . . next time. . . .

"I lost the boat, Mom," Peter says, close to tears as he
arrives by her side. "It slipped from my fingers. I couldn't
get it back." He points out over the water. "Where will it
end up?"

"Let's put on our thinking caps."

"Hmm," Peter says.

"Wait. What kind of cap are you wearing?"

"Pa's straw."

"And I'll wear a beret. Now, where will it end up?"

"Peru."

"France."

"Maine."

"Nova Scotia."

"Alaska."

"China."

"Hawaii."

"New Zealand. No telling where, I guess," she says. "There are so many possibilities."

They watch the boat until it becomes a speck, indistinguishable, as it catches the afternoon light, from the glint of a rhinestone, from a shard of glass.